THE DRAMA OF LIFE

A Study of Life Cycle Customs
Among the Guambiano
Colombia, South America

Publications in Ethnography

4

William R. Merrifield
Museum Director

Irvine Davis
Academic Publications Coordinator

Lois Gourley
Page layout

Barbara Alber
Cover design

THE DRAMA OF LIFE

A Study of Life Cycle Customs
Among the Guambiano
Colombia, South America

English translation and
ethnographic comment by
Judy Branks from Guambiano
texts by Juan Bautista
Sánchez

SIL International®
Dallas, Texas

DEDICATION

TO TOM

ACKNOWLEDGEMENTS

The cooperation of those who contributed to this book is deeply appreciated by the author.

Tom Branks, my husband, whose unflagging commitment to the Guambiano has made living among them the best years of our lives.

Ana Leonor Tunubalá, who translated the dramas into Spanish and acted as informant for ethnographic comment.

David Blood, whose illustrations catch the character of the Guambiano.

Dr. Marvin K. Mayers under whose supervision the text was prepared in English.

Dr. William R. Merrifield who meticulously edited the text and designed the original cover.

TABLE OF CONTENTS

PREFACE

We needed a storyteller. In the process of developing a primer to stimulate reading interest among the Guambiano, we decided to use a series of anecdotes from real life to catch and hold their attention. What Guambianos like best is stories about Guambianos. So we invited several of our neighbors to stop in and "talk to our machine". Some were completely intimidated by the microphone of the tape recorder; others were able to ignore it and tell delightful episodes from the past. But the color and style brought to Guambiano life by the tales of Juan Bautista Sánchez are unparalleled in any of our other materials.

He would appear at the door by night, at first out of fear of comment by the community, but afterwards to avoid a curious audience once his reputation of "storyteller for Don Tomás" began to grow. Juan adds a distinctive touch to whatever he encounters. He embellishes the typical Guambiano outfit with hats, scarves, belts, perhaps a lady's purse, plastic rainboots, or whatever his mood dictates.

We asked Juan to tell stories. It did not take long to discover that we were in the presence of a master raconteur. His narratives are rich in depth of understanding of his own culture and traits of human character. They are alive and dramatic. The following dramas were given in response to requests like "…something about the birth of a Guambiano baby." Juan would scratch his forehead, rub his hand across his mouth, close his eyes to ruminate a minute or two, then say "*Listo!*" "Ready!". He would create the dramas on the spot with a faraway look in his half-closed eyes, totally involved in his story. Setting the stage with a few well-chosen clues, he would proceed to whisper, shout, sing, play his harmonica, strum the guitar, and speak for each of the characters he conceived as he went along. Occasionally he would pause briefly to plan, then go on spinning and unfolding the scenes to completion.

Once this set of dramas was compiled, we had Juan's interpretation of the "rites of passage", or cycle of life among the Guambiano. The reader of these dramas will find himself caught up in the ongoing social sequence of life as the individuals portrayed mature and take their place in Guambiano society.

The genius of Juan Bautista can be appreciated by reading the following dramas. It is not particularly rare to find spell-binding storytellers in any culture. What amazed us at the time, and amazes us still, is Bautista's ability to create true-to-life Guambiano characters playing Guambiano roles in Guambiano scenes, and to do so on the spot. For these are not even twice-told tales. They come new and unrehearsed from the fertile imagination of an illiterate mountain farmer. We salute Juan Bautista Sánchez, interpreter of what it means to be Guambiano. He has portrayed here some of the universals of mankind against the backdrop of Guambiano life in characters so real, so much like we are, that we must laugh when they laugh and weep when they weep—warm friends, wonderful companions.

EDITOR'S PREFACE

The following sequence of "dramas" is an artistic expression in two respects. Juan Bautista expressed himself artistically as a member of a social group living out a variety of roles characteristic of their society. He has given these roles vitality and authenticity. One can enter Guambiano life naturally and comfortably through this dramatic expression. As the translator has indicated, "We must laugh when they laugh and weep when they weep", reflecting the impact they have had in her life.

It is also an artistic expression because the translator has produced not a series of folkloristic texts, rather a work of art. She has stood between the dramatist and the reader in such a way that the narrator becomes a full, rich person, reflecting a phenomenally exciting and rewarding life way. The reader has a unique opportunity of stepping into a new culture and enjoying, experiencing, being stimulated by the experience of life in that culture.

My instructions to the translator were the following:
1) Be true to the cultural expression whatever the cost. In no way cloud the richness of that culture.
2) Permit the richness of the drama, presented by Juan Bautista, to become reflected in idiomatic English. Let the reader enter

the Guambiano lifeway naturally, comfortably, as well as accurately. Let the reader sense personally through the medium of his own language the depth and excitement of what it means to be Guambiano.

3) As much as possible, allow the dramas to communicate in and of themselves. Only append material where the drama calls for it. No explanation should be an insertion, rather a dynamic expression fulfilling the drama itself.

The translator has been herself caught up in the experience. So that she not lose objectivity, the editor and others intruded from time to time in the writing process—not enough to spoil the creative urge, but enough to remind her that don Juan is the person who needs to be in focus.

The result is significant in two ways. As a translation project, the translator has achieved impact. This does not come from a "word-for-word" translation nor a "concept-for-concept" translation. She has allowed the reader to step into the shoes (or sandals, that is) of the Guambiano; to feel as he feels, to know the universe as he knows it.

The study is also a cognitive study in the best sense. The reader has an opportunity to know by the words of one of its members how he perceives his own. He is part of it, yet is an objective third party. The outsider enters the cognitive system of the Guambiano through the life experience of a member—a true guide for his own culture.

Marvin K. Mayers

INTRODUCTION

The Guambiano reservation, home of some ten to twelve thousand of Colombias indigenous peoples, is located high on the western slope of the central range of the Andes mountains. It is part of the municipality of Silvia in the Department of Cauca, near the city of Popayán. To the east, the reservation includes the Páramo de las Delicias—cold misty mountain peaks reaching above 13,000 feet. This *páramo* area is cultivated in the lower, more arable sections, and used for grazing cattle, sheep and horses. Very few live there permanently. On the north, the reservation borders the area where a larger, remotely-related tribe of Paez Indians live. On the west and south are other groups of Guambianos who have acculturated more to the local non-Indian community. Silvia, with its surrounding haciendas owned by non-Indians, is the exit to the "outside" world.

The Guambiano tribe has had 400 years of contact with this "outside" world, with the national culture, and still finds itself with its own land, costume, and language. It is a distinct group living with its own values, traditions, and religious beliefs, protected by the boundaries of the reservation.

The town of Silvia, a beautiful little village set in a valley at the foot of the reservation, is the market center for the tribe. The road recently built through the reservation has made other markets in Cauca accessible, but the merchants in Silvia provide most of the few commercial items the tribe needs. Market-day is Tuesday, and the streets of Silvia teem with Guambianos marketing their produce, buying supplies, and taking advantage of the services or entertainments offered in the town. A public health clinic staffed by Colombian medical personnel is available for assistance; dentists pull teeth; banks loan money; the Roman Catholic priest serves the people in the church on the plaza, where the Indians may be baptized or married. The Guambiano governor and his council, elected annually by the tribe, hear cases involving internal problems, particularly land disputes. Tuesday is the day when friends, family, and *compadres* meet to transact business, participate in christenings or weddings, or just enjoy each other's company. Tuesday is also the day when the Indian is forced to confront new technology, a different economic and social system, different value systems and world views. He sees things for sale that are within his grasp—a transistor radio that could bring the world to his doorstep, a water heater, hot plate, even a car or bus. The impact of this exposure beckons change in numerous areas of his life. The indigenous and national cultures confront, clash, reconcile, reject on market-day. Liquor flows, spirits and tempers rise, and the day ends for many in a state of inebriation. There has been lively social interaction; there are grave social problems.

Roads from Silvia lead to the lower villages of the reservation. A recently-constructed all-weather road runs through the major valley, up across the *páramo* to the east, opening the area to wider contact with the outside. Trails and footpaths wind across steep mountainsides reaching fields, homes, roads, and other clusters of houses. An abundance of small streams feed the main Piendamó River, which rushes from the *páramo* down the valley through Silvia to the Cauca River far below. During rainy months, the river becomes a respected, formidable force as it rages over hugh boulders, capable of taking bridges, cattle and human life in its path.

Steep, rocky mountain slopes hardly seem suitable for the economy they support in Guambia, but on them the Indians cultivate potatoes, onions, garlic, wheat and corn in sufficient quantity to feed themselves and market a cash crop. The introduction of chemical fertilizers, pesticides and irrigation have improved the

2

yield. Most families keep a horse or mule for pack animals, perhaps a few head of cattle, a milk cow, and sheep to provide wool for clothing. There may be a pig or two and chickens roaming the area around the house. Very litte hunting and fishing go on. Agriculture is the basis of the economy. The tribe's strong work ethic can be appreciated on consideration of the shortage of land, which they cultivate on seemingly impossible mountainsides. Yet this difficult land, by sheer hard work, supports an economic level envied by other peasant groups.

The climate is cool, with a mean temperature in the mid-fifties. Daytime temperatures range anywhere from 45 to 75 degrees F. Rainy seasons are cloudy and cool, while dry seasons are usually sunny and windy, warm by day, cold at night. The air often becomes heavy with a mist released by clouds scudding across the *páramo*, watering the fields with a light spray.

The most common type of house construction on the reservation is a U-shaped building fashioned from handmade mud block walls topped by clay tile roofing. The increased profits brought by better harvests, and the introduction of materials from the outside have resulted in a general upgrading of Indian houses. Today, new homes may have up to 5 or 6 rooms, with glass windows, tile floors, asbestos cement roofing—even a skylight or chimney are seen here and there.

But even in a house with many rooms and innovations from the outside world, the most important room in the house, the heart of Guambiano life, is the kitchen. Cooking is done over a wood fire in aluminum pots balanced on 3 stones, or hung on a heavy wire dropping from the rafters. Low stools, fashioned from logs, circle the fire. The warmth from the fire added to the warmth of a Guambiano family gathered around it creates an atmosphere that is hard for the adventuring youth to part from, and still harder for him to leave permanently.

Guambiano families branch out into extended kin groups living together in a cluster of houses. There are 10 major villages on the reservation, and these villages are interspersed with numerous smaller clusters of houses. A household may be made up of only one nuclear family, or many. Extended kin groups made up of children, their spouses, siblings, grand-children, widowed or aging parents—a varied combination—may be found all together under one roof. Regardless of the number of kin living in a house, both men and women are industrious in the home. Couples spend a good share of their time together working their fields. Some women contribute more to the economic status of the family than others because they have inherited land from their parents. In addition to caring for children, weaving the family's clothing, and cultivating onions, women take responsibility for making their land productive. They are respected for this by being included in a family's decisions, the respect remaining only so long as they maintain a submissive, pleasant attitude toward the man of the house. To be thought of as bossy, mean, or lazy is a gross insult to a Guambiano woman. The Guambiano man is revered as provider and final authority for his household.

As long as a household is at peace, life flows along normally, — the aged die and children are born. Sons marry and bring their wives to their father's house, where the couple work the family fields, submitting to the father's authority. In turn, the father feeds and manages the affairs of his household. It is inevitable that some sons will want independence. When a son asks for a plot of land to build his own house on, the father usually cooperates by providing materials and help. In many cases, the father and son merely add rooms to the family house, where a wife can establish her own kitchen and raise the children.

Guambiano children are a valuable source of labor. Families derive a great deal of pleasure in teaching their young children to participate in family work activities. They are taught by example rather than force, and punishment is usually only a verbal reprimand. Repeated physical punishment brings harsh criticism from the community. The atmosphere in most homes is characterized by strong underlying obligation of its members to support each other in all work. Guambiano ideals make these obligations implicit rather than explicit, and the idea of voluntary action is the basis for good relations. If a child, or even an adult, is forced to do something that turns out badly, the responsibility falls on the person who obligated him to act against his will. These and many other factors go into making a typical Guambiano home a friendly place with its share of children running in and out of doors. Grandparents, aunts and uncles, in-laws and godparents all participate in the tribe's socialization of its children.

There is a special quality to interpersonal relationships among the Guambiano that begins in the home and eventually reaches to the entire tribe. Two dominant cultural threads are woven into the fabric of Guambiano culture that form the pattern for social relationships. These two are equality and fraternity. These qualities are expressed in the language as "sameness" and "accompaniment". Guambianos enjoy being with each other. They almost never choose to do anything alone if they can find someone to do it with them. In asking for or offering assistance, the word "accompaniment" is used. A good Guambiano helps in any way he can when asked, and maintains equality, or "sameness", by asking others for their assistance when he needs help. This balance is maintained by mutual aid. An example of the daily outgrowth of these values is demonstrated in Guambiano *mingas*, or work-parties. These are held to celebrate special occasions, plant large fields, build houses, work on roads and bridges, or other projects. While they are basically intended to get work done, they also provide social contact and recreation. The person hosting a *minga* is responsible to feed his guests and their families. In turn, those who participate in his *minga* have the right to expect his assistance when they need help. This willingness to reciprocate by sharing goods and services characterizes a "good" Guambiano—one who "accompanies".

There is high regard for people and property on the reservation. Guambianos rarely lock doors unless they intend to leave the house empty for a long period of time. Theft is uncommon. However, personal ownership is balanced by the obligation to share. They readily lend to someone in need.

Guambianos are traditionally pacifists in spite of long-term struggles with the non-Indian world. They are open and friendly, pleasant, quick to laugh, preferring to maintain relationships with outsiders even when they feel suspicious. Liquor may arouse some to violence, but murder is rare. Even long-standing disputes will be temporarily put aside when the community comes together for a social event. Good will and mutual aid added to the idea of equality assure the Guambiano of his place and acceptance in his society.

In addition to social relationships provided by kin and community, the Guambiano system of *compadrazgo* provides additional social obligation. *Compadrazgo* ties are formed by sponsoring baptisms or marriages. In both cases, a sponsoring couple agrees to share responsibility with parents; but in marriages, they are expected to play an active role in maintaining peace by mediating marital disputes. Ties established in god-parenthood are serious, involving patterns of behavior long-established and respected among *compadres*. This respect for a *compadre* is manifested in pleasant greetings, hospitality, help or assistance, and the offer of a drink.

Two basic criteria in selecting godparents are careful consideration of the family's reputation, and how much daily contact their proximity might provide. Fights between *compadres* are especially odious to the community because the relationship was established voluntarily. Thus, if a family is characterized by hostility, ties with that family are avoided. Guambianos also refrain from too many *compadrazgo* ties with close neighbors which could become difficult to maintain in the process of daily contact and the obligation to drink together.

There is an intricate tension between the voluntary and the obligatory in a decision to become a godparent. The tribal value of fraternity or mutual aid is in tension with responsibility or culpability. When a Guambiano is asked to serve as a godparent, he must grant the favor in keeping with his value of "accompaniment". However, he will also be accepting social and financial obligation, sharing culpability for the child or couple he sponsors. There is a strong desire in Guambianos to avoid responsibility that might result in failure, loss of reputation, or guilt. The reader will see a delicate balance between obligation and culpability carefully maintained in the Birth and Marriage dramas, as the father negotiates with his neighbors to serve as godparents.

The same device may be noted in the Sickness and Death dramas when the Guambiano is obliged to negotiate with a shaman to handle his dealings with the world of the supernatural. The geography of the Guambiano reservation with its steep cliffs, swift river, billowing clouds, sudden storms and earth tremors, tend to enhance the Guambiano's belief in vital supernatural forces. He has myths and legends about the origin of lightning, wind, cold, mountains, rivers and lakes. He also believes in anthropomorphic beings capable of intervening in human and natural events. There are spirits which cause illness and other unexplained phenomena, and the spirits of the dead, who have power over the living for harm and death. Powerful spirits contained in any body of water are capable of impregnating human beings, but water from the *páramo* is especially powerful. Women avoid contact with water out of fear of these spirit-pregnancies. Women must also be kept from contaminating others during menstruation. It is the blood from menstruating women, or those who have just given birth, that angers the spirit world. Contamination by "dirty blood" can cause various illnesses or even death. Rituals performed by a variety of qualified shamans restore equilibrium between man and the spirits by cleansing contamination or dismissing the spirits of the dead from family dwellings. The tyranny of the shaman can be seen throughout the dramas, but particularly during sickness and death. The balance of obligation and face-saving devices is very evident as the man of the house negotiates with the shaman in the Death drama.

Some pivot points of Guambiano life, with its systems of beliefs and values, are portrayed in these dramas. On the surface, some of the particulars are exotic, but time after time, we are compelled to reflect on our own customs and on the similarity of the values which underlie them. Then it is easy to see ourselves in these whose history and development have been so "other" than our own, but who are so profoundly "like" us.

BIRTH

Conception and birth among the Guambiano are accepted as normal phenomena of life. Only the abnormal requires explanation, and this is attributed to supernatural powers. Men as well as women may be impregnated by water spirits, but for men such pregnancies would be fatal because of their inability to deliver. Miscarriages, abortion, abnormalities and occasional infanticide can all be rationalized by "spirit pregnancies".

Very few concessions are made for pregnant women. The Guambiano woman's skirt, fashioned to accomodate an increase or decrease in size, effectively masks the coming event. The subject of pregnancy is handled with discretion and discussed only in the immediate family. During this time, women are euphemistically referred to as "sick". They usually work right up until delivery seems at hand. A few days before delivery, some families call in the shaman to perform a ceremony over the woman in order to keep evil spirits from entering her body or harming members of the household during her period of contamination.

Today, there are many changes occurring in the practices surrounding the birth process, due to long exposure of the tribe to national culture, the road which provides easier access to clinics or hospitals, and extension programs in pre-natal care. Some women restrict their activities and diet for a period of time before delivery. But this is not a widespread practice, and others will even try to precipitate labor by climbing the mountain and returning with a heavy load of firewood.

There is no special place set aside for birth. The woman usually wants to be near the fire to keep warm. She kneels or squats on old clothing, gunny sacks, or a cowhide, and may grasp a rope tied to the rafters. The husband and other women of the household are usually on hand to support the wife, but the actual delivery is left to a midwife. There are several of these in each village, some who have received limited training from an extension worker, and others who qualify only because of long experience. The umbilical cord is tied with yarn and cut with scissors or a knife. When the placenta is delivered, it is buried in or near the house, sometimes sprinkled with ashes or wrapped in an old piece of cloth.

The mortality rate in childbirth is still high. Failure to pass the placenta is a common cause of death. Midwives have limited knowledge and no emergency facilities for coping with the abnormal. The shaman may have had some exposure to medical training and access to drugs, but too often he is unable to handle emergencies either. So it is understandable that women manifest a fatalistic attitude toward delivery. The non-Indian community offers clinics and hospitals, but this world is still feared or mistrusted by the majority of Guambiano women. The value of accompaniment is also violated in a hospital situation. To die away from home is a most terrible fate.

When a baby is born, it is swaddled in lengths of old clothing and placed in a hammock made from a meter of blue wool flannel and two ropes. The shaman comes immediately to cleanse the house. For the next forty days, the woman is confined to her house, limiting her activities and eating only special foods prepared by other members of her family. At the end of this period, the shaman again comes to cleanse the woman and her household, announcing to the community that the contamination period is over and the woman may resume normal work.

There are different ways of handling the christening of the newborn. Sometimes families christen the child at birth by sprinkling water over him. This is done to safeguard against the event of the child's death before he can be taken to Silvia for baptism in the church. In other instances, the father and another woman of the household take the child to Silvia before the mother's confinement is over. They look for god-parents to serve on the spot. This can present difficulties in getting anyone to accept, since the godparent is required to pay for baptismal clothing and certificate. He is also expected to supply liquor for the celebration. Most Guambianos are not immediately prepared to assume either the expense or the responsibility. Some families like to ask non-Indians from Silvia or even foreigners living in the area to serve. In spite of the Indian's suspicion of outsiders, he feels that their financial position is superior and ties of obligation less crucial. If the father can't find someone to serve, he will then look for Guambiano families from towns other than his own, to avoid situations that might lead to friction or conflict.

Christening day in Silvia is not without cross-cultural clash as the event-oriented Guambiano is obliged to get his family and godparents together for a previously-scheduled christening in the church in Silvia. Now that the reservation has been opened up by the road, norms are changing rapidly, and the whole day is more pleasant for everyone involved. New mothers can accompany the christening party to Silvia and return home comfortably by bus.

THE DRAMA OF BIRTH

Characters:

Husband	*Hu*	Other woman of household	*OW*
Wife	*Wi*	Manuel	*Mn*
Midwife	*Md*	Manuel's wife	*MW*

SCENE I

Inside a Guambiano house, a woman is in labor. Her husband is instructing another woman of the household to find and bring the midwife.

Hu: It looks like the time has come for my wife to have her baby. She's in quite a bit of pain. Please go call the midwife so we're not caught unprepared. It's important for you to find her right away.

OW: All right, I'll go now.

Hu: If she's home, please have her come straight over here.

OW: If I find her, I'll bring her back.

Hu: Don't waste any time. Tell her to come right away. I don't know for sure that my wife is ready to deliver, but we can't take any chances. I'll feel more secure when the midwife gets here. She knows what to do. It's impossible for me to be much help. Wife, how do you feel?

The woman of the household leaves to find the midwife...

Wi: The pains are coming faster. I think the time has come. I'm not sure how much longer I'm going to live.

Hu: Don't talk like that. Now that we've called the midwife, everything is going to be all right. Just pray to God for help. It's the only thing to do right now. I don't think He would let anything happen to us. Let's wait for the midwife.

The midwife arrives and calls at the door...

Md: Good afternoon!

Hu: Come right on in.

Md: I got your message and came right away to see how things are going. The woman said your wife is in a lot of pain. I was just outside my house weeding the onions.

Hu: Thank you for coming. We were getting a bit frightened before you arrived. That's why I sent the woman to bring you over. Please attend to my wife if you can stay. She has so much pain that I think she must be about ready to deliver. First of all, though, come over here and have a cup of coffee. Then you can take care of my wife.

Md: Thank you. I don't think there's anything to get excited about right now.

Two hours pass. The delivery is safely accomplished and the husband converses with the midwife about post partum care of his wife...

Hu: Well, we're all so very happy and relieved that my wife has safely delivered a normal baby, thanks to you. We appreciate what you've done for us.

Md: That's quite all right.

Hu: Now maybe you could give me instructions about the diet my sick wife should follow. Will you please tell me how to go about feeding her now?

Md: Sometimes a sick woman continues to have pain. If this happens, send for me.

Hu: I will. Since you're so close, you could just come over.

14

Md: Of course. Take good care of your wife. Your daughter knows how to take care of things like this. Now then, you can dress the baby and everything will be in order.

Hu: Good. I don't think it's a good idea for my wife to walk around just anywhere before the household has been cleansed, do you? That needs to be taken care of too. Also, before the month is over, we'll need to take the child to Silvia for christening.

Md: That's a good idea. You should be prepared. Babies are very delicate and can pick up all kinds of diseases. Be very careful that he doesn't die before you have him christened.

Hu: You're absolutely right. We'll take the baby for christening before the month is out.

Md: Good! Because people say that if a child dies before it is christened, the parents are to blame for what happens to its soul. So you'd better have him christened as soon as you can.

Hu: Yes, thanks for that good advice.

SCENE II

Several days later, the husband and wife are planning the child's christening and confronting problems in choice of godparents...

Hu: Listen, wife, shall we try to find non-Indian or Guambiano god-parents? What do you think? It will cost us more if we choose Guambianos.

Wi: I think we'd do better to look for non-Indians. You know a few of them personally, don't you? Take your time choosing and make sure they're the kind to keep a promise so we don't run into trouble the day of the christening. They may back down at the last minute, you know.

Hu: I'm aware of all that. I'll feel better when I have everything arranged.

Wi: I know. Don't you think you should get it done today?

Hu: All right. I'll go now. I should be back soon. I have two friends I can ask since I have to find someone quickly. I'll also need to talk to the priest about what day to go down to the church in Silvia.

Wi: Then look for non-Indian godparents in Silvia. It all gets too expensive with Guambiano godparents! You know how it goes. Every time you meet each other, no matter where you're going, you have to stop and drink together. You drink up our money instead of spending it on food that the family needs.

Hu: I know, I know! What are we going to name the child? We should decide and have the name ready in case the priest asks me for it. I sure do hope before the month is out that you'll feel up to taking the baby to town yourself so that I don't have to ask someone else to do it.

Wi: I'd like that as much as you would.

Hu: I hope by the end of the month we can all go to town for the christening.

Several days pass...

Hu: Wife, what do you think I should do now? The non-Indian couple that promised to be godparents sent word today that the man is sick.

Wi: We might have known! Then we'll have to look for Guambianos.

Hu: Maybe I should talk to Manuel.

Wi: Do you think he might do it?

Hu: I'll just keep asking until he agrees. His family are all very nice, sincere people. They've always been good neighbors. Do you think I should ask them? They have a good reputation. Now that our arrangement with the non-Indians has fallen through, I think I should insist on Manuel's family being our godparents.

Wi: Well, why don't you go ahead and ask them, then.

Hu: All right. I'll go over to Manuel's right now.

Wi: Good, but before you leave there, be sure they're really going to do it. Keep after them until you have their word.

Hu: I'm going to insist until they promise me they'll do it. I have a feeling they'll accept. This isn't as big a responsibility as asking them to be godparents for a wedding. I'm going over right now and see what they say.

Wi: Good. See you later.

SCENE III

The husband arrives at Manuel's house carrying a bottle of rum. It is late in the afternoon and Manuel is just returning from his field. The husband calls at his door...

Hu: Hello. Manuel, are you home?

Mn: I'm here. Come on in!

Hu: Thanks very much. I came looking for you. What a surprise to find you home.

Mn: Well, here I am.

Hu: I came to ask you a big favor.

Mn: Come on inside where we can talk.

Hu: Thank you.

Mn: Sit right down over there.

Hu: Thanks very much. I came to offer you a drink. I'm afraid you're not going to like what I have to ask you.

Mn: Wait just a minute. Maybe I should call my wife so she can be in on this conversation. She was out weeding the onions a while ago right around the house while I was in the cornfield. I'll go call her.

Hu: That's a good idea.

Mn: I'll be right back.

SCENE IV

Manuel finds his wife outside in her onion patch...

Mn: Come here, wife. A man just came to the house.

MW: Who is it?

Mn: Someone looking for us. That's why I came to get you. It looks like something you should be in on.

MW: Don't you know what he wants?

Mn: Come on inside so we can both talk to him.

MW: Just a minute. I'm almost finished here.

Mn: The man said he came to ask a favor, and I thought you should hear what he wanted before I agreed to anything for both of us.

MW: Of course.

Mn: Let's go.

MW: All right, I'm ready.

SCENE V

Manuel and his wife enter their house to talk to the waiting husband. The wife greets him cordially and then withdraws to sit down apart from them, as polite women do in the presence of men...

MW: What a miracle to have you here in my house!

Hu: Yes, I guess it is a miracle. I came to visit you.

MW: How nice that you could come.

Hu: I came to ask you a big favor.

MW: You did?

Hu: I'm embarassed because I'm afraid you won't like what I have to say, but I'm offering you both this liquor and ask you to serve as god-parents for my new baby.

Mn: Let's see what my wife thinks. Do you hear him, wife?

MW: Yes, I hear him.

Mn: What do you think? This man is asking that we do him this favor.

MW: You know what everyone will say. You know they'll say it's wrong if you refuse to carry a baby for christening when someone asks you to. I think we'll have to agree to be their godparents. But you decide.

Mn: All right then, since this man insists, we'll serve as godparents. We'll go down with the baby on Tuesday.

Hu: Great! Thank you. You're the only ones I had any confidence in. I was embarassed and afraid to ask anyone else. I have so much confidence in you both. Thank you. I can't tell you how relieved I am that you agreed.

Mn: That's all right. As I just said, we'll both go down with you and the child on Tuesday. Just in case we don't get there on time, go ahead and put our names on the list when you get to the church.

Hu: Right. If we get there before you do, I'll have everything ready with your names on the priest's list. Please don't forget to come, even though we don't set up an exact time right now.

Mn: We'll leave home early in the morning and wait for you in Silvia.

Hu: See you in Silvia, then. You be ready when we get there.

PUBERTY

The rite of passage from childhood to adulthood is celebrated only by female members of the Guambiano tribe. The first menstruation for a girl must be announced to the community, not only because she is now marriageable, but also because she now has new power to contaminate. The family must take proper steps to provide for her cleansing.

A small, round hut is constructed by the girl's father, where she must spend four days in isolation on a special diet. During this time, her activity is restricted to spinning wool or hand-weaving small carrying-bags from hemp fibre. At the end of the four days, the mother prepares a basin of water mixed with four special herbs with which to bathe the girl. She then dresses her daughter in new clothing and takes the old to the river to wash. The family sends for the shaman to cleanse the girl and the house before the girl is permitted to resume daily activities.

A *minga*, or work-party, is called to plant a field in honor of this occasion. This also serves to demonstrate the girl's new standing and economic power in the community. Family and neighbors are invited afterward to a dinner and dance, at which time the girl serves each of her guests a glass of rum, an act signifying her new social position and responsibilities in the community.

21

THE DRAMA OF PUBERTY

Characters:

Father	*Fa*	Daughter	*Da*
Mother	*Mo*	Shaman	*Sh*

SCENE I

In a Guambiano home, the father has just discovered that his young daughter is menstruating. He looks for his wife and finds her in the kitchen...

Fa: Did you know that the girl is having her period? What are we going to do now?

Mo: Yes, she told me.

Fa: Then we'd better get busy and make arrangements to have her cleansed. They say it's not good to ignore the cleansing rituals.

Mo. Of course it's not good. There are medicines we'll have to get for her and we need to build a special little hut to put her in.

Fa: That's right. Now then, we'd better get busy on that hut.

Mo: That's your responsibility and you should get at it right away.

Fa: I should start lining things up.

Mo: You should get right at it. There's no reason to wait any longer.

Fa: I should look for roofing straw first.

Mo: Yes, go ahead and get that taken care of.

Fa: I wonder if there's any chance of finishing it today anyhow since we need straw, branches, and rope for tieing it all up.

Mo: Oh, it isn't that big a job. We can finish it today. If you need help, let me know. If you want to cut straw now, I'll go along and help you carry it.

Fa: Good. Can you go right now?

Mo: Yes.

Fa: All right, let's go right now. The girl should stay in the house. She can get the soup and coffee ready for lunch.

Mo: (To daughter...) We're going to the field to cut straw. You fix lunch for us.

Da: All right.

Mp: Go ahead and put the soup on too.

Da: Yes, I'll take care of it.

Mo: We'll be back soon, so don't wait too long to get things on to cook.

SCENE II

The mother and father work together in the field cutting and gathering straw as quickly as possible...

Mo: Do you think we'll need one or two sacks of straw?

Fa: It's better to cut two while we're at it. You can carry one bag back and I'll take the other. You gather up now while I cut.

Mo: All right. Cut quickly and I'll follow you and gather it up.

Fa: Good. I think that's enough straw now. Tie it up so we can get back home.

Mo: Why don't you do that, since I can't work as fast as you can.

Father ties the bags and hoists one onto his back...

Fa: Wait a minute, this straw is really heavy when it's green. I don't think you can carry it.

Mo: Let me see. Yes, it sure is heavy, but I'll carry it anyhow. Otherwise, I'm afraid we won't finish today.

Fa: Yes, we really should get moving.

Mo: Let's go then.

They set out down the trail for home...

Mo: Whew! This load gets heavier every minute.

Fa: If it gets too heavy, set it down and I'll come back for it.

Mo: No, it's not far now. I think I can carry it the rest

of the way.

Fa: Good, we're almost home.

Mo: Don't worry about me. I'll be all right.

SCENE III

Back at the house, the couple chooses the site for the hut right outside their house and begins construction. It is around noon...

Mo: How many poles and rafters do you think we'll need?

Fa: Three poles and twelve branches to bend around the sides.

Mo: A simple little hut shouldn't need so much wood.

Fa: Well, we'll see. I have that rope I brought home from our place down in hot country sitting around here somewhere.

Mo: Where is it?

Fa: Out behind the house. Go get it.

Mo: I'll see if I can find it.

Fa: Hurry up or we won't get this finished in time.

Mo: I'm just as worried about that as you are. All right, here it is. You're the one who knows how to do all this, so why don't you just keep on working. I'll go inside and see what the girl is doing.

Fa: Go ahead. If she has the coffee ready, call me.

Mo: Lunch will probably be ready soon.

Fa: Just go see if the coffee is ready. I'm hungry. It's way past lunchtime.

Mo: All right. I'll go in and see how things are coming.

SCENE IV

Back inside the house, the family eats a hasty lunch together...

Da: Come on, Father, the coffee is ready.

Mo: Yes, come get it while it's hot.

Fa: I'll be right there.

Mo: Here, drink your coffee, it's ready. As soon as you finish, don't you think you should get right back to

25

work? I'm so worried that we're not going to get finished before dark!

Fa: I'm worried about the same thing. When I finish the hut, we have to keep the girl in it for four days. That's what has to be done, whether we like it or not. Daughter, you stay right here and don't leave the house.

Da: I'll be right here.

Fa: Wife, you come now and help me. I want to finish up quickly. It's hard work doing everything by myself.

Mo: All right, I'll be right there and stay with you while you work.

SCENE V

Back at the hut site, the afternoon wears on as the construction takes shape. There is a great deal of pressure to finish before dark...

Fa: Please hand me those poles.

Mo: These?

Fa: Those right there. I'm going to tie them on quickly.

Mo: It looks like you've finished the framework.

Fa: Yes. Now you can start passing me the straw.

Mo: It doesn't look to me like two bags is going to be enough.

Fa: It will have to be enough. We're not going to make a perfect roof for four days. Now pass me the straw so I can start putting it on.

Mo: This is really a lot different from building a house. You're tieing everything all the way around.

Fa: That's because it's a round hut. Now it's going faster. I'll have this ready soon. Please hold it right here while I get it tied.

Mo: There.

Fa. This piece of rope sure is stiff.

Mo: Give it to me and I'll go wet it. Just a second.

Fa: Do you have it?

Mo: Wait a minute!

26

Fa: I need it right now! If you don't hurry up, we're not going to get finished.

Mo: Here you are.

Fa: Do you have an old clay pot you're not using? I want to cover the point of the roof so rain won't come in through the hole.

Mo: I'll go see what I can find.

Mother vanishes into the house and reappears a minute later...

Fa: Did you find something?

Mo: Here.

Fa: Pass it up. I want to see if it fits.

Mo: Here, take it.

Fa: Oh, I need something. Pass me my machete so I can cut this pot down a bit.

Mo: Just don't drop it. Cut it carefully.

Fa: Don't worry. I've got a good grip on it. Well, everything is ready! Call the girl! She should eat and drink something. We're going to have to leave her here in the hut for the night.

SCENE VI

Back inside the house, the mother gets her young daughter ready for her four-day confinement in the hut. She displays concern for the girl in practical ways, knowing the nights will be cold, dark, and full of unnamed fears for the girl.

Mo: Have you eaten?

Da: Yes.

Mo: Then you'd better come along now. You'll have to stay in the hut without leaving, you know, so bring your skirts and shawls to keep yourself warm. I'll come see you during the night to make sure everything is all right.

Da: Yes, please come, Mama. In case it gets really cold,

27

you could bring something more to cover me with.
I'm going to get cold out there.

Mo: Yes, I'll bring you something later on and stay with
you for a while.

*They walk together outside toward the hut. The father calls to
them...*

Fa: It's six-thirty. You must go inside the hut now.
Today is Monday, tomorrow Tuesday, Wednesday,
then Thursday it will be all over.

SCENE VII

*Four days have passed. The family is gathered at the hut to complete the rest
of the prescribed ritual which will include a ceremony performed by the shaman...*

Fa: Now that the four days are over, we must call the
shaman to perform the purification rites. We'll ask
Trino to do it for us. First, though, we have to bathe
the girl. Wife, you must find all the medicinal herbs
and boil them in a pot for the washing ceremony.
You must gather *rram rrol, pishi calo, cuchig cun,* and
yem tsig. (Herbs used by the Guambiano for which
they have no Spanish names.)

Mo: Yes, those are the medicinal herbs we've used for
purification since I was a girl.

Fa: And those are the same ones you use to wash the
girl. When she has finished her bath, we'll call Trino.
But she still must not leave the hut except to urinate.

About an hour later...

Mo: We're ready for Trino. Did you find him?

Fa: Yes, he's here.

Mo: Please bring him over here. There you are! Trino,
our daughter has reached puberty and has had her
first period.

Fa: I thought about letting it go without all this ceremony,
the way so many do today, but they say it's a big
mistake not to do everything the way the

28

tribe has always done. So we went ahead and built the hut. Now that the girl has finished her four days of isolation, she's had her bath. We've done all we're supposed to, and now I want to ask you a favor, Trino. Could you purify her for us?

Sha: Oh, that's not hard to do. I'm qualified to do the purification rites. Please prepare the woven purse.

Fa: What do you need in it?

Sha: These five things: herbs, rum...

Fa: How much of the herbs do you need?

Sha: Three *huevos*. (*Huevo*, Spanish for egg, indicates a measure about the size of an egg.)

Fa: All right, and how much rum?

Sha: One bottle of regular rum and one bottle of your home brew. Now give me the woven purse with all the things I mentioned and I can get right to work.

Fa: Wait just a minute until I get everything together.

Sha: All right.

Fa: Be sure to sprinkle the medicine with your mouth or your hand everywhere the girl has been around the whole house. Trino, you know all about these things. Should you purify us all at the same time?

Sha: Yes, of course. Don't you worry about a thing.

Fa: I appreciate it. Wife, you must wash all the girl's clothes. Be sure you do it yourself. Don't ask anyone else to do it for you.

Mo: Of course I'll wash the clothes myself. There's no reason for me to ask someone else to do it. This isn't something I want talked about outside the family.

Fa: That's right. As the mother, you are responsible for the girl's dirty clothes. After the girl is bathed, you must wash the dirty ones she wore while she was menstruating. Later, when everything is all cleaned up, Trino can do the purification rite for her.

The family gathers back at the house for the ritual cleansing of the house and its occupants...

Fa: Trino, everything is all ready.

Sha: Good, I've just cleansed all the areas where the girl has been lately. Since the whole house is contaminated, I have to cleanse you too.

Fa: Then I ask you to cleanse us too.

Sha: Very well.

Fa: Please cleanse all of us with the medicine.

Sha: Of course. This is for everyone now, not just the girl. I'm going to cleanse you by sprinkling the medicine all around.

Fa: Do whatever you have to.

Sha: Now then, everything is finished.

Fa: I can't thank you enough, Trino. Please wait just a minute. I have a little rum left in my bottle. Drink it as a reminder of the cold nights. It's just a little glass.

Sha: Thank you. Everything is finished. Thank you.

Fa: It's good to have everything taken care of properly. Menstruation is such a normal thing for women, there's no excuse for fathers to let it go unnoticed. We fathers should be careful to take care of the women's purifications, because they don't know how to handle things like this for themselves.

Sha: Yes, this is our responsibility as men of the house.

Fa: Naturally fathers are the ones responsible, because women don't know how to take care of these matters. By the way, tomorrow I'm going to have a *minga* (work-party).

Sha: Oh, good!

Fa: Yes. People say it's a big mistake not to have a work-party to celebrate a girl's puberty. If we don't have one for her now, later on when she has her own home, she will want to have work-parties and the people won't come. My deceased parents used to tell me that if everyone does things properly according to all the puberty customs, then people will gladly come help when the woman has a work-party of her own later on.

Sha: You're absolutely right, I'm sure. They say this is the way to do things right.

Fa: Trino, you'll come tomorrow and help prepare the field for planting?

Sha: I'll be glad to come. When are you going to get together? In the afternoon?

Fa: Yes, to dig the rows. The men will dig rows while the women plant the potatoes. It isn't going to be a big work-party. I'm hoping we can finish the work in one day. It depends on how many come. We'd like for you to be here so everyone will know the proper ceremonies have all been taken care of. You'll join us, Trino?

Sha: Yes, I'll be there. Good night.

MARRIAGE

Most young couples in Guambia find satisfactory way of getting to know each other even though "dating" is considered improper and generally not permitted. The community tends to disregard the activities of young couples unless they become serious and decide to get married, or the girl becomes pregnant. In such cases, the young people may go to their parents for supervision, or the parents may not know anything about the predicament until they are informed by the community.

Parents react in different ways when confronted with a possible marriage, but in most cases the family discusses it freely from many points of view. Although parents may suggest a partner to a young person, there are very few cases where children are forced to marry against their wills. Once a young adult chooses a partner, the parents consider the match in light of the other family's social and economic position. Parents would not be in favor of a daughter marrying where the boy had no land, thinking that marriage would be his only way of obtaining it. Family reputation is another consideration. An unfriendly or uncooperative family makes for a difficult marriage. Then too, the family must consider its relationship with its potential in-laws for possible future disputes. It is important to avoid a situation that is likely to create friction.

The custom of trial marriage is no longer common. If the parents of both girl and boy disapprove of a marriage, the couple may elope. However, since they eventually have to make a home with their parents, disapproval is a strong deterrent. Many couples do not know each other well before they marry; abandonment is another social ill.

Once parents and young person reach an agreement, contacts are made between the couple's parents. When they have settled on marriage, the boy's parents accompany the couple to Silvia to secure necessary papers, usually under cover of night to protect the couple from comment. The girl then returns to her home until the evening before the wedding, where the boy may visit her under parental supervision.

The boy's family also takes the initiative in arranging and paying for the wedding, assisted by other relatives who live in the community. Because of the heavy social and financial responsibilities entailed, the family must rely on this help from family and friends. The father of the groom must find suitable godparents, a process complicated by the serious responsibility taken on by such godparents. The father must organize the wedding *minga*, or work-party, gathering and purchasing food for the dinner and dance. All wedding festivities are hosted by the groom's parents without involving the bride's family in any way. Once the father of the groom has arrangements made, the date can be set with the priest in Silvia. The time lapse between the boy's announcement to his father of his intentions to marry and the actual wedding day may be less than a week.

The day before the ceremony, a small party made up of bride, groom, groom's parents and the godparents walks or rides the bus down the mountain to Silvia. The couple has already secured necessary papers on a previous visit to town, seeing to it that everything is officially ready for the wedding day. Now they return to the church to make an appointment for the ceremony, say their confession to the priest, and pay for his services.

Early the following morning, after a night in a local hotel, the bride, groom and godparents dress for the wedding. The bride's skirt is bleached white wool, handwoven in the same manner as her everyday skirt, but decorated with blue stripes. Her shawl is bright red or pink wool flannel, adorned with as much as eight to ten pounds of white glass beads and, occasionally, an hierloom silver cross. Her hat is borrowed for the occasion, as only a few wedding hats still exist in the area. Its design dates back to the Spanish colonial period. The groom's wedding poncho is the same white handwoven material as the bride's skirt, also decorated with horizontal blue stripes, and the godparents wear similar outfits. Both women may have on as many as three skirts, heavily pleated across the back, weighing up to five pounds, and giving a decidedly rounded appearance. Beautifully arrayed, the wedding party then proceeds to the church where the priest performs the ceremony and records the marriage.

After the ceremony, the party returns to the hotel in Silvia to prepare reception tables for guests who will arrive in the forenoon. The tables are laden with bottles of liquor, wine, homemade *chicha* or corn liquor, cigarettes and cookies purchased in town. The wedding party seats itself in a room near the tables as the guests file by. Each guest receives a cigarette and cookies, as well as a drink from the host and godfather. Congratulations are offered to a bride and groom so shy and embarassed that they pull their hats down and tuck their heads into their ponchos to hide their faces. Those passing by outside the house during the festivities are also invited inside to accompany the party.

Meanwhile, as the ceremony takes place in Silvia, the rest of the groom's family hosts a wedding *minga* in the fields of the groom's father. It is hoped that the yield from this planting will offset the heavy financial burden the family has had to bear in connection with the wedding. While the men are in the fields, the women are in the kitchen at the groom's home peeling potatoes, preparing onions and corn for the wedding feast. If the family owns animals, one may have been slaughtered to provide meat for the soup. Since all the guests who come to the house must be fed, preparations are elaborate, demanding many hands. Anyone on the reservation who chooses to come is welcome. It is considered proper for the bride's parents to come late in the evening for the feast, but only her mother and father. It would be in poor taste for them to bring other relatives of the bride. If they do not choose to attend, then food is sent to them at their home. Guambianos gather from all points of the reservation to celebrate a wedding, but those who are more socially aware do not bring children or others who cannot contribute in some way to the fiesta.

Late in the afternoon, back in Silvia, the group takes the bus back up the mountain. Before the road was constructed through the reservation, a wedding party would climb the trail accompanied by flutes and drums. In those days, it was common for the party to stop briefly at the home of the bride to greet her parents. Now, the musicians meet at the groom's home for the wedding supper which begins as soon as the party arrives from Silvia.

The music begins around nine o'clock and guests arrive bringing gifts of rum or home-made corn liquor. Everyone who comes to the house is served coffee, bread, and a bowl of soup made from potatoes, corn and perhaps meat. The value of "accompaniment" comes into play at a wedding feast in that no one is allowed to go unfed. The musicians play as the room fills with guests and soon the food and drink, the warmth of the fire, and pleasant social contact stir up a festive spirit. Dancing beings.

Later at night, the party is interrupted when the groom's father, the host, calls the couple apart to a separate room to give them his counsel and to lecture them on proper behavior in the family. The godfather begins his role as counselor, along with other respected members of the community who might wish to give advice to the young couple. The newlyweds are instructed in their duties to each other and the family. This session officially ends the day for the young couple and they are free to take leave of the party and retire.

Dancing may continue until dawn back in the main room of the house where, unfortunately, the good will of the party is often broken by drunken disputes and fist fights. Dawn finds many of the guests stumbling homeward, or sleeping off their drunkeness along the roads.

The bride and groom will spend the day after the wedding with the girl's family and possibly work a piece of the father's land to demonstrate their continued loyalty and good will toward the bride's family. However, the bride is now officially established as a member of her husband's family and must submit to the authority of his parents. She owns her own land, inherited from her family, but her services are now rendered to her husband's family. The couple will work the father's fields and, in turn, he takes responsibility for their room, board, and general oversight. If problems arise which the father cannot control, he may appeal to the Guambiano governor for a ruling. Internal family disputes are handled by the governor and his council. In many cases, the governor may advise a couple to separate from the groom's house. The groom's father must then give them a plot of land and help them with materials for their house. Once a separate house for such a couple is completed, family relations improve. They have forfeited the father's protection over their affairs, however, even though their loyalty and service continue to him.

THE DRAMA OF MARRIAGE

Characters:

Boy	*Bo*	Godmother	*GodM*
Boy's Mother	*BM*	Godfather	*GodF*
Boy's Father	*BF*	Boy's Uncle	*BU*
Girl	*Gi*	Relatives	*Rel*
Girl's Mother	*GM*	Musicians	*Mu*
Girl's Father	*GF*		

SCENE I

In a typical Guambiano home, a boy has just told his father of his intentions to get married, and asks his parents to go with him to ask the girl's parents for their consent. The father and mother make preparations for the customary visit to the girl's house. It is evening...

BF: My son tells me he's found the girl he wants to marry. It looks like we'd better go talk to her parents. Get your bag ready so we can go soon. Bring along four bottles of rum so we'll have enough. Hurry up. I'd like to get there around nine o'clock. You too, son. Get yourself ready so we can leave. Is everyone ready?

BM: Yes, we're all set.

BF: Good, let's go then. Go on out while I lock up. We won't be back before morning. Of course it all depends on how your girlfriend's parents receive us. If everything goes smoothly, we should be able to bring the girl home with us and go on to Silvia. Come on, let's get going. It's quite a way to her house and we're going to be tired when we get there. You'd better bring along a bottle for us to drink along the way. It will help us relax and not be so nervous in front of your girl's parents. Did you bring one?

Bo: Yes.

BF: Let's keep moving. It's a long way. We're going to

39

be worn out by the time we get there. Son, I told
you to bring a bottle for us. Did you?

Bo: It's right here!

BF: Let's hurry along. Now, let's rest a minute. I'm so
worried about whether or not they're going to open
their door to us. Son, did you make firm plans with
your girlfriend? Did you tell her for sure what night
we'd be coming?

Bo: Yes, everything is all arranged.

BF: I'm still worried because there are people who
change their minds and won't open their doors at the
last minute. Are you sure you told the girl to be
ready to open her door?

Bo: Of course! Relax.

BF: Let's drink this bottle of rum. We'll just have to
wait and see. I'm going to quit worrying now that
you've assured me you've worked out all your plans
together. Let's finish up this bottle. Drink a little,
son, so you won't be nervous.

Bo: Thanks.

BF: O.K. Let's keep moving.

SCENE II

*The boy and his parents arrive outside the girl's house. It is dark and quiet. It
is likely that the girl's parents will be taken completely by surprise with the whole
turn of events, not knowing anything about the couple's relationship. But the girl is
watching for the boy and his family...*

BF: Oh, no! They must have gone to bed already. I
don't hear a sound and the lights are out. Son, you
go take a look. Did you tell the girl you would call
at her window?

Bo: I'll go see. She told me she would wait for me
tonight. You stay here. I'll go give her the word.

BF: Get going! Hurry up!

The boy goes to the girl's window and calls...

40

Bo: Open the door.

Gi: Did you all come?

Bo: Yes. I just got here with my parents to find out how your parents are going to feel about us getting married. What do you think they'll say when you tell them we want to marry and live together?

Gi: Relax. They just went to bed a few minutes ago. Go to the door and call my father. If he doesn't answer the door himself, I'll come and open it.

The family goes to the front door and the father begins calling...

BF: Good evening! (no answer) Hello! (no answer) Anyone home?

GF: Good evening. Who's out there?

BF: It's us!

GF: What do you want?

BF: We've come to see you about something that has to do with my son. We'd like to talk to you about his marriage and make plans with you. We must talk together. Please open the door.

GF: Open the door quickly!

BF: (To his family...) They've opened the door!

GF: Please come in.

BF: We'd like your permission to come in and talk to you for a few minutes.

GF: All right. Come inside. We'll get stools so you can sit by the fire.

BF: (Aside, to his wife...) Good, both mother and father got up. And the girl is taking care of us as guests. It looks like everything is going to be all right.

BM: (Whispers back...) That's good!

BF: My son tells me that he has found the girl he wants to marry. It is a well-established custom for the parents of the boy and girl to get together and talk things over. We've come to see what you have to say about all this. My son tells me that he and the girl have been friends for a long time and now they'd like to get married. The customary thing to do then is talk to you and hear what you have to say either for or against this marriage.

GF: I didn't know a thing about any of this. I don't even know if they're engaged!

BF: It's a disturbing thing the way some young people do things these days. But our children have not been either deceitful or rebellious. We want to reach an agreement between us as parents of this couple to help them do things properly.

GF: Yes, I'm only too aware of the way things are done nowadays.

GM: It doesn't look like there's much we can do now. They've decided to get married of their own free will. We'll have to face it sooner or later.

BF: Of course. They've decided to get married and now we parents ought to reach an agreement. This is the way things are done. It would be a serious matter not to accept the children's decision. It is our place to encourage them.

GF: You're right, of course.

BF: Please get the bottle of liquor out, son. Did you bring a shot glass?

Bo: Yes.

BF: Good. Let's all drink together!

GF: Now just a minute. Let's not get in a hurry. We can't accept your drink until we're sure how our daughter feels about all this. Daughter, it's your turn to talk now. What are your plans? If you're serious about this decision, we want to hear what you have to say. Please call your boyfriend over here. I want to talk to him, too.

BF: (To wife...) Tell him to come here. Sit right down here, son.

GF: Until tonight, I didn't know a thing about you two. I didn't even know you were seeing each other. I have no idea if this is the first time you've come around our house to see her, or if you've been meeting secretly, or if you've even made a definite decision yourself.

Bo: Then I'll tell you. I've made my own decision of my own free will. That's why I came here with my parents. We want to marry and spend the rest of our lives together.

GF: All right. It looks like you've made your decision. Daughter, what do you have to say? Do you promise to live with this boy until the day you die? Yes or no?

Gi: Yes. I asked him to come talk to you tonight.

BF: Now that we've heard the girl's decision, there shouldn't be any further question about the matter. So let's have a drink!

GF: Thank you.

BF: Here, have this little bit to start with.

BM: Thank you.

GF: This is your bottle, not mine, but I'd like to serve you if you'll permit me.

BF: Please do. While we've been talking, it has gotten late. It's midnight. Tomorrow we need to go down to Silvia with the couple to get their marriage license and papers. We'd like for you to have the girl get ready to go home with us now.

GF: (To girl...) Go get ready.

BF: We'd like to take you with us right now.

GF: You've made your own decision and now you have to go with them.

Gi: Of course, father. I'll go right now and get ready.

GF: Hurry up!

BF: My goodness, it's two o'clock. I want to be in Silvia by dawn so people don't notice us and start talking.

GF: Right. If you don't have any problems in Silvia, please bring my daughter right back home. If possible, bring the boy for a visit, too.

BF: Thanks very much.

SCENE III

The boy and his parents pay a visit to Trino's house intending to ask Trino and his wife to be godparents for the wedding. It is a day or so after papers have been secured for the marriage...

BF: (Calling at the door...) Hello! Hello! Anyone home?

GodF:	Come on in. Who is it?
BF:	It's us. We came to ask your hospitality.
GodF:	Come right on in. What's your problem?
BF:	We've come to ask you a big favor. It has something to do with my son. I know it's going to be a big favor. But everyone has to ask for help sooner or later. I'm asking you and your wife to be godparents for my son's wedding.
GodF:	Oh, I don't think we could do that!
BF:	But you know very well that we never make problems for our neighbors. My son just said to me this morning, "Father, please ask Trino and his wife to be godparents for me." The couple want very much for you to be their sponsors. This is why I'm here now asking you.
GodF:	Oh, it just isn't possible. Why don't you see if you can find someone else.
BF:	It really isn't such a big thing to ask. Have a heart for the young couple. We really don't want to ask anyone else. It's you we want. It isn't possible to have a marriage without godparents. You're the only ones we want to ask and we would like to settle this with you before we leave here.
GodF:	I already told you. I just can't do it. Wife, what do you think about all this?
GodM:	I don't have much to say about it. It's up to you to decide. You know how people say it's a bad thing to say no to someone asking a favor. You shouldn't say no to the couple. But you do what you think best.
GodF:	I always do what I think best!
BF:	Let's have a drink and seal the bargain!
GodF:	Hold on there. I never said I'd do it. You might be wasting your drink.
BM:	But you just can't refuse us.
Bo:	I don't know anyone else to ask. That's why I brought my father here.
GodF:	All right, then, we'll serve for you. Like my wife said, it's not good to refuse someone who asks you a favor. We'll accompany you and the girl to Silvia.
BF:	Good! Now that you've decided to be godparents,

we'd appreciate it if you'd be responsible for picking up the girl and getting her to Silvia with us for the wedding.

BM: Please take care of that for us, will you?

GodF: Yes, we'll go get her.

Interlude: The day before the wedding, the Father addresses his household as they prepare to leave for Silvia later in the afternoon...

BF: The wedding day has come. Everyone get ready to go to Silvia. We'll leave early in the afternoon, since it's not necessary to go at night. It doesn't matter what people say about us today. What we're doing today is a common, ordinary thing—going to a wedding!

SCENE V

The godparents are on their way to Silvia for the wedding, and stop at the bride's house to pick up the girl. Her parents see her to the door...

GodF: They told us that we should come here and pick up a girl at this house.

GF: That's right. The couple has made their decision to unite their lives. Now, as their godparents, you're supposed to see that she gets to Silvia for the wedding, and then bring her back to our house for one last visit. When the wedding is over, everyone is invited to stop here on your way to the groom's house. We'll wait for you here after the ceremony.

GodF: It's very nice of you to invite us. We'll have to wait and see.

GodM: See you later.

GF: All the relatives are invited to stop back by the house after the wedding, too.

*The bride's parents turn back into their house, knowing that they will **not** be included in any of the ceremonies, and that **no one** will stop by the house on his way to the feast.*

45

SCENE VI

Back at the groom's house, the same day before the wedding, the family is getting ready to go to Silvia, as the father makes arrangements with his brother and the household to take care of the minga...

BF: This afternoon we'll be leaving for Silvia to be there for the wedding ceremony tomorrow morning. Now tomorrow, before we get back to the house, you take care of the *minga*.

BU: Yes, I'll stay here at the house to supervise things.

BF: We have to have this *minga* to help defray the cost of the wedding dinner. We've got a big job ahead of us. When the Guambianos have a wedding, it's customary for us to get together and invite our friends and relatives to help with the work. That's why I'm calling on you to give us a hand.

BU: Right.

BF: Tomorrow, I'd like for you all to spend the night here. I don't want anyone to go home tomorrow night. This is the only night I'm asking you to do this for me.

Rel: We'll be glad to help.

BF: The next day, too, I ask that you stay until the guests leave. We'll have a simple lunch for you before you go.

Rel: Thanks very much.

BF: With your help, we can handle our son's wedding properly. When the boy told me he wanted to get married, we knew what our responsibilities would be as his parents for the wedding. We want a proper wedding for our children.

BU: Of course you do.

BF: After the ceremony tomorrow night, when everyone comes to the house to eat, we must invite the guests to have a drink first. I want you all to help take care of everyone. This is the only night I ask you to do this for us.

BU: Yes. We surely don't want anyone to leave saying that he wasn't offered a drink. This way, we can see that everyone is taken care of. All of you who are responsible for the guests do your best to see that no one is left out when you serve the food too.

BF: This reception is a big responsibility and I'm grateful to each one of you for your cooperation. At ten or eleven o'clock tomorrow night, we're going to begin serving drinks at the table. The people will complain and criticize us if they don't all get served at the table. That's why I'm asking all of you to be on your toes. You can help out all day, beginning with the *minga*. But tomorrow night, you who are helping us serve the others, have a drink first. Then you can go serve the others. First of all, be sure you take three glasses to the ones who are at the head table, the wedding party. There will be four of them to receive three drinks apiece.

Father continues at length with detailed instructions for the family.

SCENE VII

The house is teeming with guests, relatives and family all participating in the wedding festivities the night after the previous scene. The bride's parents have arrived for the wedding supper and dance...

BF: I am honored to be your host tonight. Let the music begin! Play the flute and drum! The newlyweds are going to dance. Everyone get ready to dance when the music starts. Here, have a little drink before you being to play.

Mu: Thank you.

BF: Please start the music so the bride and groom and their guests can dance.

Music plays

BF: Everyone dance to the sound of music. This party is for everyone to enjoy. The couple is going to dance four times. After that, everyone is free to dance again. Play the flute!

Music plays

BF: That's the way I like to see things. Dance all night with that kind of enthusiasm! I'll be here to serve you. Go ahead with the music, with the flute and drum. The couple is going to dance again.

Music plays

BF: The groom's parents and the godparents are all going to dance a welcome dance with each other. Let the music go on. Everyone join in with good spirit!

Music plays

Mu: We'd like to rest a while.

During this part of the fiesta, the main dancers are the bride and groom, his parents and godparents. They carry lighted candles and dance in separate lines facing each other. Four dances are completed with the 3 couples. The rest of the guests join the festivities when the formal dancing is finished.

SCENE VIII

In a room apart from the wedding party, the bride and groom are called apart and seated on a bench, flanked by their godparents, while the family elders charge the couple with their new responsibilities. Proper behavior, reinforced by the shame mechanism, is included in the counselling session...

BF: All right, my children. You've united your lives into one, and I'm your father. The girl has a new father. We are the ones responsible for you from now on. Each of you has your own father and mother. Both of you must respect your own parents, boy and girl alike. Not only in word, but in deed.

BU: You'd better pay attention to what he's saying.

BF: The girl's father is no longer responsible for you. We are the ones in charge. I am now the girl's father and my wife is her mother. Now my son's wife must obey. She must not offend us either in word or deed. Submit to your husband because he is the head of you both. And you, son, also must take care of your wife, because she should be treated as you would treat your mother.

GodF: That's right!

BF: Be very careful in your marriage, because it is a blessing from God. Now, as a couple, you should govern yourselves by helping your parents, visiting them, and if possible, giving them little gifts.

GodF: I agree!

BF: This is the best way for you to do things. There's no better way than what I've just told you. But if you disobey or disregard this advice, I'm not responsible.

GodF; You both ought to follow his advice carefully.

BF: I am giving this advice to avoid problems as father of a married couple. If you disregard my counsel, I'll have to refer the problem to the authorities.

GodF: That's right!

BF: And you won't be able to make fun of the authorities the way you do your parents. The council will come and punish you severely in front of all the people. I didn't exert any pressure on you to get married. You both did it of your own free will. And now you must submit to my authority as head of this house.

BU: This is the way to live. If we don't obey good advice when we get it, who is going to straighten us out if we get into a mess? We'd better use our heads so we don't have problems in the future.

BF: Be careful that you don't have to be brought before the council. Life is complicated. This is the way you should live. If you don't obey my counsel, I can appeal to the governor to punish you. Then the authorities will punish you on my orders in front of all the people. Because of disobedience, you will be publicly shamed. The governor is the final authority in this tribe, and he can make your lives very difficult. After a while you will learn to behave better. This is the only way to take care of things. This is why we older folks give you advice before any problems arise, to help you avoid them. When the council has to come settle a dispute, it's the boy's father who has to go and say,

"My son is behaving in such and such a way... Please come, Mr. Governor, as judge, and restore this marriage. Because my children are rebelling against me and have disobeyed, they deserve to be punished according to our laws. As their father, I give you my authority to punish them. Now they are under your orders."

You two listen with both ears, because the governor has final authority over you. That's all I have to say.

After this lecture, the couple is free to retire while the fiesta continues as long as anyone remains sober enough to celebrate.

HOUSE BUILDING

New homes are appearing all over the reservation today. The decision to build a new house may be based on several different factors. It may be that the old house is falling apart and not worth repairing. The family might be outgrowing the old structure and need an addition for a son and his family. Perhaps the most common reason is the wish for independence as married couples reach maturity. Whether or not dissension arises within the extended family group, a husband and wife eventually wish for their own kitchen fire as a symbol of their ability to handle their own affairs of life.

When a son reaches the decision to build a house, the father must decide which plot of his land is most suitable. If they are only going to build an extension on the old house, it is still customary to invite the shaman to apply his powers of divination to the location to determine whether or not it is free from tunnels made by the underground spirit *loru*. To build a house over one of the spirit tunnels is to invite all sorts of detrimental occurrences to the family who presumes to live in such a location. Another source of danger is the site of an old *Pijáo* grave. The Pijaos are believed to have occupied the area of the reservation before the Spanish conquest—a powerful tribe whose spirits are still feared by the Guambiano today.

After the shaman puts his stamp of approval on a site, the owner of the land contracts a *maestro*, or building supervisor, to oversee his project. The family begins making adobe blocks, gathering poles and beams, bringing tiles or roofing up from Silvia—a process which may take months or even years to accomplish. The dry season is the best time of year to build.

The male members of the household usually get the four walls laid in place before they ask for help from the community. Then finishing and roofing are done at a *minga*, when the family, friends, and neighbors are gathered to help. Anyone who might have dropped by to help at any stage of the building is also invited to the *minga* supper, along with many others who come to get the roof finished in one day.

There is a light-hearted atmosphere about a housebuilding *minga*. It is usually scheduled for a Saturday when the week's work in the fields is finished. Those who gather work seriously for intermittent periods, then stop to socialize, tease, joke, and jibe each other with good-natured comments. During the work on the house, the women are busy peeling mounds of potatoes, preparing onions, perhaps meat—everything that will go into the soup for the evening meal. They enjoy being together, sharing the latest news. Everyone who comes to work on the house is fed and given enough food to take home for his entire family. The repartee in the final scene of this drama gives a most delightful glimpse into the heart of the ideal Guambiano. He interacts with his fellows in an attitude of neighborliness and good will. The host is esteemed as gracious by the community because he has previously accompanied them in their projects, and they are now reciprocating by attending his *minga*. Shared responsibility for one another through times of prosperity as well as economic stress is part of the bond which has held them together against odds which have caused other tribes to disappear.

THE DRAMA OF HOUSE BUILDING

Characters

Father	*Fa*	Shaman	*Sh*
Sons	*So*¹ ² ³	Father's Brother	*FB*
		Helpers	*H*¹ ² ³

SCENE I

A Guambiano father is sitting around the fire with his sons talking over plans for beginning construction on a new house. They discuss how they will divide the cost of the project...

Fa: We need to come to some sort of agreement with you boys about this matter of a new house. The place is in such bad shape that people are going to start wondering what's wrong with us. I think we should all agree to get a new house built and go look for a builder right away. What do you think?

So¹: We're with you on it. There are plenty of men in this family, but we sure haven't taken much interest in keeping the house in good shape.

Fa: That's for sure! All right, then, let's start by gathering the materials we'll need—adobes, wood—everything we need.

So²: Fine. We need to think about starting from scratch with a brand new structure. If we try adding on to this one, it will probably fall right down. Imagine how ridiculous we'd feel if that happened!

Fa: We'd better get started then. I'll go see about getting adobes made and buy wood while you get the rest of the things together. I need you and your mother to cooperate with me in this project so people won't start talking about us. I'm going to see about getting adobes. You get the roof tiles and see about wood. We'll need to talk with a builder. That's the most important thing right now. We'll need to begin gathering food to feed the workers, too.

55

So¹: Oh, that's right!

Fa: Now that you're all grown men, you can help me build our house.

So¹: With your good advice and direction, we'll all work together to get the job done. We'll get our money together and have all the wood ready. We really should see a builder about drawing up a plan. Father, you tell us what to do. We'll do everything to help in any way we can with the things you need us for.

Fa: If we don't get things rolling ourselves, it's a sure thing nobody else is going to. When we get to the actual construction, the people will help us. But we can get things started ourselves to begin with.

So²: Sure, it's up to us. We're with you. You're the one to tell us how you want things done.

SCENE II

Plans are beginning to shape up for the new house. The men have decided it's time to send for the shaman to help them decide on the best location for construction...

Fa: Who's out there?

Sh: It's me!

Fa: Well, come on in!

So²: Sounds like Don Gregorio is here!

Fa: Tell him to come on in to the kitchen. There you are! Come on inside. We asked you to come, but didn't expect you so soon. Glad you could come.

Sh: I had to make a trip to the other side of the village anyhow, so I stopped by to find out what you need from me.

Fa: Thank you very much. We want to ask you something. Let's go sit down in the kitchen. Here's a bench.

Sh: Thank you.

Fa: Have a cup of coffee.

Sh: Thanks. That's a good cup of coffee.

Fa: Thank you for coming over. I want to ask you a favor, Gregory. I'm thinking about having a *minga* for my sons so they can build a new house. Since the first day we started talking about it, they've been working on plans. But we wanted to consult you first of all. Too many times a great deal of work is done in vain and ends up in problems because people don't have a purification ceremony before they start building. This is why I sent for you.

Sh: Well, my good man, now I understand what this is all about. It certainly is not a good idea to build a house without some careful consideration of the location.

Fa: That's the way I feel. I think that's the reason so many people have trouble after a house is built. Strange things sometimes happen. The first thing I want to ask is that you cleanse the building site.

Sh: My good man, is that what you called me over for?

Fa: If you have time, could you come over again later on and do this work for me?

Sh: I just don't know, right now. Tonight I'm invited to another house. How about tomorrow?

Fa: If you could come back later tonight, I could have everything you need on hand for you to start as soon as you get here.

Sh: The first thing I'll have to do is check my sensations to see what they tell me about your location.

Fa: Ah, yes. What do you need for that—herbs, tobacco, rum...

Sh: Let me think. One measure of herbs, five dollars, two packages of tobacco, a pack of cigarettes and a bottle of rum. This job is going to take time. It will take me from around seven o'clock or so until about ten-thirty to figure out the best building site for you.

Fa: I see. We can take care of getting everything you need.

Sh: Fine. If you can get all the things I mentioned by tonight, and wait for me, I'll come back later and take care of this for you.

Fa: If you'll do this for me tonight, we'll have everything ready. Please do come if you can.

Sh: Don't worry about it. I'll be back.

The shaman leaves the house. The family converses around the fire...

Fa: Well, I'm glad he agreed to do the job for us. We should ask him to concentrate especially on the two locations we've picked out. We'll have to see what he says about them, whether we should build on the upper or lower part of our lot. We'll have to make our plans after we see which spot he chooses.

So¹: Right.

Fa: When it comes to the actual building, it's just too much work for two or three of us. So I want to reach an agreement with our neighbors to help some with the job.

So¹: Yes, you should make arrangements for more help. Just levelling the lot goes awfully slowly when there are only a few people working on it.

Fa: Two or three men can't get much of anything done by themselves.

So²: That's precisely why we should have a *minga*.

The father and his sons continue discussing things as an hour goes by. Darkness falls and presently the shaman returns...

Fa: Is that you back already?

Sh: Yes, I'm back. Do you have my *jigra* (ritual carrying-bag containing shaman's fee) ready?

Fa: Yes, it's all ready. Where would you like to begin work?

Sh: I'm going to sit outside on the left side of the house. The best method is to stay on the left side. If you have my *jigra* ready, please pass it here.

Fa: Here it is. The money, tobacco, everything you asked for is in there. Now please concentrate carefully on what your senses tell you about the two locations.

Sh: Of course. I'll work until I find the exact spot for your new house. We need to know which of the two sites is the best, is that right? In order to learn this secret, I'll have to work hard to discover if the upper or lower end of the lot is best.

Fa: Please do whatever you need to do. If you need me for anything, just call.

Sh: If I should happen to need you, what time do you go to bed?

Fa: Around nine o'clock.

Sh: Well, I'll be here until at least ten-thirty. It's going to take a great deal of effort and hard work on my part to discover the right spot for you.

Fa: Well, if you need anything, call me.

Sh: While I'm working over on this side of the house, don't open the door or light any candles. It disturbs my concentration to have living spirits around. I'm trying to discover if there are bad spirits lingering around here and I don't want to be disturbed. Don't open the door on this side of the house at all. If I call, come out the other door on the right side of the house.

Fa: We'll do that. Now, if you need anything, just call me.

Sh: Good. You might just stay up until I do call you.

Fa: Sure, we'll stay around for a little while.

An hour or so passes...

Sh: Oh, good, you're still up!

Fa: Yes.

Sh: Can you come over here a minute?

Fa: I'm coming.

Sh: This bottle of rum isn't going to see me through the night. One little bottle just isn't enough. The problem here is turning out to be a tough one.

Fa: For goodness sake, we have more rum. We'll get you another bottle right away. Shall I bring it to you now?

Sh: Yes, bring me a full bottle.

Fa: I'll be right back. Here you are!

Sh: Pass it over here.

Fa: I filled it right up to the top.

Sh: Good. Another full bottle should see me through.

This whole issue is turning out to be bigger than I thought.

Fa: Is that so!

Sh: We'll see. I've just discovered part of the secret in my divinations.

Fa: Keep up the good work!

Sh: If the rum holds out, I shouldn't have any problems.

Fa: I certainly hope not. Do you need more tobacco?

Sh: No.

Fa: Herbs?

Sh: No. All I needed was more rum. I don't know why you thought I could work out a problem like this on just one bottle in the first place. You can go to bed now.

Fa: Right. Sorry!

Sh: If I need you for anything else, I'll call you. Go ahead and get your sleep now.

An hour or so later, the family dozes inside the house...

Sh: Are you all asleep?

Fa: Oh, Oh, no, we're awake!

Sh: Come here!

Fa: Everyone up quickly, he called us!

Sh: I want everyone out here.

Fa: Wait just a second until we get awake. Here we are.

Sh: Come over here. Is the whole family here?

Fa: Yes, we're all here.

Sh: I want you to know that on the lower side I discovered a tunnel belonging to the spirit *loru*. You can go ahead \and build there if you want to, but your hard work will all be in vain.

Fa: We'll do exactly what you tell us and build only where you say it's safe.

Sh: That's why I'm telling you all this ahead of time. In the upper section of the pasture around the big rock, I haven't found anything dangerous. I don't see any signs of graves ever dug there or anything that would forbode evil in the future. In that location, I find no reason for either adults or children to have any problem. But in the lower part, you'll find the spirit tunnel of a *loru*. There are people who build houses right over these tunnels, but eventually they end up tearing everything down. If you build a house over this spirit tunnel, the whole family will eventually die. It's just not a good idea to build over spirit tunnels. So I'll tell you before you start anything, that the upper site in the pasture near the big rock is the exact spot for your construction site. I have tried very hard to find out everything I can and I feel that this is your problem-free location. My strongest sensations come from the right side. My vibrations tell me that the other site, the lower end, will bring danger or complete failure. This is why you should build near the big rock. That's the best place to consider for your house.

Fa: Good. That settles it! We'll plan the house for the area behind the big rock. That's the best spot. It's fairly level there already.

Sh: If possible, I'll come back and show you the exact spot when it gets light.

Fa: Yes, it would be better if you could come back and show us the precise location your divinations have indicated.

Sh: If possible, I'll come. What day are you planning to begin work?

Fa: Probably on a week-end, on Saturday. We're having a *minga* to get all our friends and family together to see if we can't finish the job all in one day. It might be possible. I don't think there's a lot of levelling to do. It's fairly flat.

Sh: Then the work should move along quickly. Perhaps I can help.

Fa: By all means, if you can, please come and join us.

Sh: I'm going home to bed now. I've lost a lot of sleep.

Fa: That sounds like a good idea.

Sh: Yes. I'll be back tomorrow.

Fa: We'll send you a message when we settle on an exact day for the minga.

Sh: Good. I'll come help.

Fa: Great! Thanks a lot!

SCENE III

*Several months go by. The day of the **minga** arrives. At the construction site, the father and his brother host the day. As helpers arrive, they offer gifts of food to their host to help feed the crowd. The host responds very formally, expressing his appreciation by using the diminutive form in Guambiano to heighten the formal tone of his speeches...*

Fa: It's wonderful that so many of you could come. I appreciate it!

H¹: Maybe this little bit will help you out.

Fa: Oh, thank you so much for the bread!

H²: Here's a little *panela* (raw sugar) and a few rolls.

Fa: How nice of you! Everyone gather around over here. Everyone join us now. Please check with the supervisor to see where he wants you to begin working. I'm sure all of you know about building a house. So you can each help in the part you like to do best.

FB: Those of you who stay down on the ground, be ready to pass the rafters up to the workers on the roof.

Fa: I can't tell you how much I appreciate your help. Everyone gather around now and let's get to work. My brother will help you get started while I take care of the others who arrive later.

H³: Perhaps this little gift will be useful to you.

Fa: Thank you. I appreciate your coming. Why don't you join the others over there. I'm a little short of money, but we decided we need a house anyway. Thank you for your gift. It helps me out. Please join us over here.

FB: Thank you all for coming. We'll spend the whole day together and get this job done.

Fa: Those of you who came to work on construction, please go with my brother and begin on that. The rest of you can help with other things. If you need someone to cut wood or pass something up to you, just call on one of these people to help you. Thank you.

FB: Thank you for coming to help us.

Fa: I know it's asking a lot, but we'd like to see if we can finish up the house in one day. Now that the walls are up, I think we can do it.

FB: We're asking everyone to help all you can so we can finish by nightfall.

Fa: Yes. It looks like everyone is all set.

FB: The owner of the house is going down to Silvia for some last-minute things we need, so I'll supervise while he's gone.

Fa: Yes, I have to go to Silvia. I forgot a few things we'll need to finish up the job here, and I'll pick up some more groceries while I'm there. I'm leaving things in your hands, brother. You can supervise and work with all these wonderful helpers until I get back.

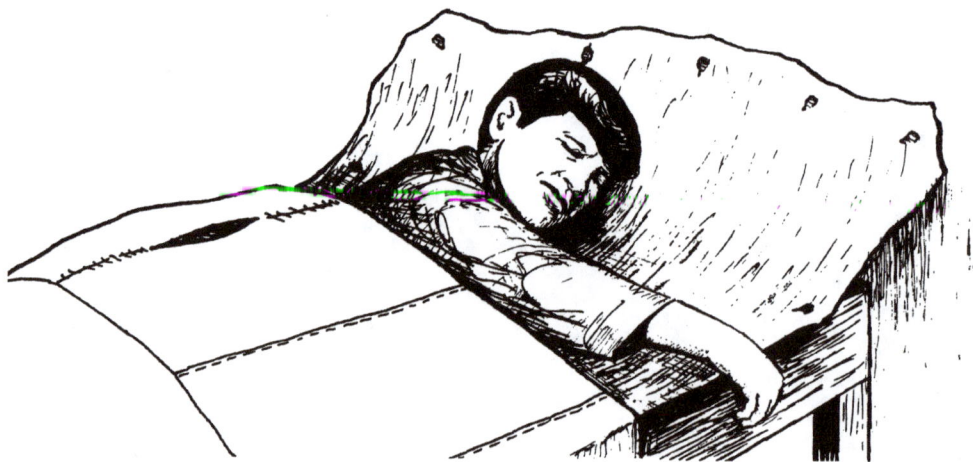

SICKNESS

The standard in Guambia is to have everyone and everything "cleansed", after becoming contaminated, as a precaution against spirits inhabiting the whole reservation. The greatest concentration of spirits lurk around bodies of water and in the high mountaintops of the *páramo*. Homes, tools, clothing and people must be ritually cleansed by a shaman four days after each woman in the household begins menstruation. A contaminated person makes these spirits furious. Although they cannot enter the human body, they may inflict pain or cause illness. Anyone going to work the fields in the *páramo*, or mountaintop areas, while a woman in the family is contaminated will inevitably arouse the wrath of the spirits.

Shamans are called in both to perform prophylactic ceremonies against harm from the spirits, and to cure the many illnesses they cause. The wide range of ceremonies and techniques are learned from many sources. Some curers are herb specialists, others use techniques of massaging, and today some have even learned to use antibiotic drugs and give injections after a period of training in the national culture.

The repeated reference to the "left" and "right" indicates some orientation for good and evil that the shaman utilizes as he appeases the unseen. The origin of this orientation is not clear, but it is obvious that "right" is good and "left" is bad. The authority of the shaman as mediator between man and spirits is still undisputed among the Guambiano.

THE DRAMA OF SICKNESS

Characters:

Father	*Fa*	Son	*So*
Mother	*Mo*	Family	*Fam*
Shaman	*Sh*		

SCENE I

Inside a Guambiano home, a family is gathered around a very sick son. The shaman has been called in to diagnose and cure the case...

Sh: What seems to be the problem here tonight?

Fa: Our boy has come down with something. It looks like he might have a high fever. During the night last night he was out of his head saying all sorts of crazy things.

Sh: I wonder what could be causing all this? I'm so sorry. It does appear to be a strange illness.

Fa: I don't know what could have brought it on. He went to bed like he always does. But around 10 o'clock he began to feel funny. He said he was too hot, so his temperature must have been going up about that time. The next thing I knew, he was out of his head saying funny things like,

> "Bring me my hoe. I left it in the field where I was working. My hat, too. My dog, my faithful companion drowned in the river!"

I told him no, the dog was sleeping right by his bed and nothing had happened to it. But he just kept on saying all sorts of strange things.

Mo: What do you think could have happened? Shaman Manuel, I wish you would divine what your feelings tell you about all this so we'll understand his problem. In a case like this, I guess the first thing to do is get herbs and have you go to work.

Sh: Of course! You're absolutely right. It's vital that

67

someone divine the sensations in cases like this.

Fa: That's exactly what I was thinking, too.

Mo: It's probably a *duende* (spirit).

Sh: Why do you say that? Where has the boy been lately?

Mo: He went to the *páramo* a couple of days ago. He told me he went out by the lake. That night he started to seem ill, and by last night he was babbling deliriously. It could only be a *duende*, since he was up on the *páramo*.

Sh: There's no question about it! A *duende* got him! My goodness! Bring me some herbs, and I mean bring them right this minute!

Fa: (To mother...) Look for herbs and tobacco quickly! Oh, we don't have a drop of rum in the house!

Sh: Just bring me herbs and tobacco then, if you don't have any rum.

Fa: We have no way of knowing when something like this might happen and we just didn't buy any rum.

Sh: Things like this happen when you least expect them.

Fa: (Calls to Mother...) Do you have the *jigra* (ritual bag) ready?

Mo: I'm getting it ready right now.

Fa: Bring it here immediately.

Mo: Here it is. It only has herbs and tobacco.

Sh: That's all right. I'm going outside now.

Mo: Would you like a bench to take out with you?

Sh: Yes, if you have one you could lend me.

Mo: Take this one. You'll need a poncho to put over you too. It gets very cold out there at night.

Sh: If you have one handy, I'll take it. I'm going out to divine the secret of this whole situation.

Fa: Please do all you can to try and discover what your senses tell you about this problem.

Sh: I will. You two stay around and take care of that sick boy.

Fa: Of course. We'll stay right here by the sick boy. You go ahead outside.

The shaman goes outside for an hour or so, then returns to the family to talk to them about the boy...

Fa: I just don't understand it. How could such a thing happen to us? Now the boy is nauseated. It's more likely a *duende* pestering him since he's just come back from the *páramo*.

Sh: My dear man, I know from experience that a *duende* can pounce on people like lightning if they're angry about something. Not just children, but adults too. Do you know whether or not he's been around a contaminated house?

Fa: My daughter just finished her period, but we didn't pay much attention to it around here. That's why the boy went off to the *páramo* without asking about contamination. He doesn't know any better when it comes to these matters.

Sh: I can't believe it! You people are just unreal! Don't you understand yet at your age that NOBODY can walk around the *páramo* when he's contaminated? Now wouldn't it have made more sense to have told him his sister was menstruating so he could have been cleansed before he went to the *páramo*? Wouldn't it?

Fa: Oh, this younger generation. I don't know what we're coming to. The way the girls "forget" to let me know when they're contaminated. I guess it's obvious that it was a *duende* that got the boy.

The shaman leaves the house in disgust to continue his divinations. He calls to the father a few minutes later...

Sh: Hey in there!

Fa: What?

Sh: Come out here a minute!

Fa: I'm coming!

Sh: Sit down here with me for a few minutes.

Fa: O.K. I'm sitting.

Sh: Right over here beside me. Now that I know that you people traipse all over the *pàramo* even when you're contaminated, I understand why the *duendes* are so furious. I might as well tell you straight out

69

that your boy escaped being struck dead on the spot by the skin of his teeth. He was able to run for his life and get back home safely. These girls of yours must be taught to tell you when they're menstruating so that the purification rites can be performed before anyone leaves the house!

Fa: I know you're right. But they just don't tell me.

Sh: The *duendes* don't usually deliberately harm the average person. They don't have to because in certain places where they live, a normal person knows better than to presume to walk around contaminated. This is the spirit that brings on this kind of sickness.

The father and shaman re-enter the house...

Mo: The boy has diarrhea and is vomiting now.

Sh: I can see just by looking at him that he's worse. You'd better get the things I'll need to work over him right now.

Fa: We just don't have anything. We're caught completely unprepared by this illness.

Sh: Of course you are! Do you think it might have anything at all to do with the fact that recently you have all been ignoring the ritual ceremonies we're supposed to do for you? This is the very reason you don't have the things you need for this emergency. Isn't it true that you've been so healthy you've forgotten to take necessary precautions I could have done for you?

Fa: You've got the picture.

Sh: You poor, foolish people! Well, for right now, I'm going to chew the herbs you gave me and do what I can for the sick boy. We'll see how he's doing by morning. According to what my sensations tell me, my feelings are strong on the right, not on the left. This means that the illness isn't fatal. My senses almost escaped from my right side, but in the end, they stayed there. I don't think his illness will get any worse after tomorrow. Now in the morning, I want someone from this house to get right down to Silvia and buy herbs, tobacco and rum.

Fa: I won't have to be told that twice! I'm going to see that everything is taken care of properly like I should have been doing all along.

Sh: Oh, I know how you people are. You just go your own way until someone dies.

Fa: I'm scared now that something even worse might happen. We need to get things taken care of quickly to see if we can do something to help the boy. All of you get your money together so I can buy herbs and rum for this household.

Sh: Yes, it's the responsibility of the whole family to help one another.

Fam: You're right.

Sh: Once you get everything together, call me right away. Do you have to be away from the house today?

Mo: No. I'll work right around the house. I had plans to go to Altares, but I won't go today. When my husband gets back with the herbs and rum and medicines, we'll call you right back. Do you think you could come back tomorrow night for a purification ceremony? Or better yet, this afternoon?

Sh: A lot depends on how things go after what I've already done for the boy. It might be possible for me to return when you have everything I need ready. We'll see.

Father and the shaman walk toward the door...

Fa: I beg you to come back and do this ceremony for me. I'm leaving for Silvia at the crack of dawn for the things you need.

Sh: All right. Send me word the minute you have everything ready. Our houses are close, so just send word when you get home from Silvia. But be sure you have enough of everything—four measures of herbs, five cigarettes and two bottles of rum. Get one bottle of the real stuff and one bottle of contraband. You can put this in the *jigra* for my fee.

Fa: I'll do everything you say. We'll let you know when we're ready.

71

Sh: Send word the minute you get back from Silvia.

Fa: I implore you to come and get things straightened out for my household.

The next evening, after the family has gathered all the items required for a proper purification ceremony, they send for the shaman again...

Sh: Open the door! I'm here to do another purification on the boy. What's going on here?

Fa: What do you mean?

Sh: Where's the patient?

Mo: Oh, I moved him over here. It's dark in this corner.

Sh: Well, well, what's happened to you?

So: All I know is that I went up on the *páramo* to work. About noon I began to feel sick, sort of dizzy and headachey. If the house had been any further away, I'm not sure I could have made it home.

Sh: What do you know! The reason you're sick is because you were walking around the *páramo* all contaminated. You just can't play around with the *páramo*. You cannot walk out of a contaminated house, and by that I mean when the women of the house are menstruating, and go to the *páramo*. It's a wonder the *duende* didn't strike you dead on the spot.

So: I understand that now. What a dope I was. Nobody told me the girls were menstruating. It was my turn to go take care ₁of the cows and I just left without giving it a second thought. Around noon I started feeling queasy. I didn't even feel like walking. My head ached and my whole body hurt and felt weak. So I hurried back to the house.

Sh: Well, the *duendes* must have been having a fit. These things always happen when you're not cleansed. So you be careful that you don't walk around up there again if you're contaminated. You must insist that the girls in this house let you know when they're menstruating.

So: It's hard to believe all this happened just because they didn't tell me.

Sh: I'm really sorry about that. But the bad spirit is on my left side. I'm going to begin work again. My divinations never fail me and they indicate that the sensations are on the right side, the good side.

Mo: You are so wise in all these matters. Please tell the patient what he should do.

Sh: All right. Don't go outside.

So: Right. I'll stay right in the house.

SH: It's obvious that the *duendes* have been harsh with you. I'll have to work to make them happy so they'll leave you alone.

Fa: That will certainly be a relief!

Sh: Stay here while I go out a minute.

Fa: Of course. If you need anything, just call me.

Sh: I'm going to sit out here for the ceremony. Don't fall asleep too early. Around nine, I'll call you in case I need something.

Fa: We'll stay up until ten o'clock.

Sh: Don't light any candles on the side of the house where I'm working.

Fa: Right.

Sh: Later on, I'll come in and look at the patient to see how he's doing.

Fa: Fine.

Sh: I have to purify the patient 3 times with medicinal herbs. Then I must do my divinations outside to find out what's going on. After that, I'll come back in and continue working on the patient.

Fa: You just go ahead and do whatever you have to do.

An hour or so passes...

Sh: Hey!

Fa: What?

Sh: Open the door. I'm coming in to do a ceremony over the patient.

Fa: Good!

Sh: Where's the boy? I can't see anything, it's so dark.

Mo: He's over here

Sh: You all stay on my right side. How are you, boy, better?

73

So: Yes.

Sh: How did you feel after the ceremony I did with the herbs?

So: I felt fairly well. I don't have such a headache or as much nausea. But I still feel very weak and sick.

Sh: I'm sorry to hear that. I'm going to perform the part of the ceremony where I blow over you four times with medicine. Sit up.

So: If I can. Will someone please help me up?

Sh: Make yourself comfortable.

So: How's this?

Sh: Sit like this, please. Now you stay here on the left side. I'm going to blow from the right. I want everything done from my right. Four times on the right. After that, I have to try to perk up the *duende's* feelings and blow four times on the left side. O.K. I'm finished.

So: Thank you so much.

Sh: We'll see if you don't feel better now. This ceremony usually makes people feel stronger and ready to sleep. If you feel like you want to, go ahead and drift off to sleep in peace.

So: I will. After all you've done for me, I have hopes of getting better.

Sh: I'm going outside now, but I'll be right back in. It depends on what the spirits are doing out there.

So: Good.

Sh: Where's the rest of the family?

Fa: Over here.

Sh: I'll be calling you a bit later. Keep the patient comfortable and covered with his blankets. I've purified him with the medicines.

Fa: Thank you.

Sh: I'm going outside again to think about whether or not I should give him medicine to take orally, too. If I think it's necessary, I'll come back in.

Fa: Good. We'll wait for you.

A few minutes later...

Sh: Bring me a cup of water.

Fa: How much?

Sh: About half a bowlfull. I'm going to prepare a medicine.

Fa: Here's the water.

Sh: Grind up these herbs very fine on a rock.

Fa: Right.

Sh: Find a flat rock and grind them up. Don't lose any of the powder. When it's ready, bring it here so I can put it in the bowl.

Fa: O.K.

Sh: Hurry up, now!

Fa: Here, it's ready.

Sh: Fine. Please get me a spoon to mix it with. And I mean a clean spoon. We'll see what results we get with this liquid I've mixed. My sensations are still telling me that this whole matter is on the right, not on the left. It's likely that the patient will improve steadily. I really feel that if he takes this medicine, he's going to get better. If the mixture doesn't make him vomit, it will be a pretty good indication that he's going to recuperate quickly.

Fa: I hope you're right.

Sh: However, if he begins to vomit right after he takes this, it will indicate that the results were no good. But I'm fairly confident that this won't be the case. Let's go give him the medicine.

Back inside, the house is very dark...

Sh: Where are you?

So: Right over here.

Sh: Take this medicine. You need to drink all of it.

So: I will.

Sh: Take it all!

So: Thank you.

Sh: Finished?

So: Yes.

Sh: You drink every bit of that, right now!

So: Oh, all right!

Sh: I'll be back in half an hour to see how you respond to it.

Fa: Good. I'll wait up for you.

Sh: If you feel like sitting up, fine. If not, go to bed.

Fa: The boys can wake me up if I fall asleep before you get back.

Another hour passes. The shaman returns to the patient's house...

Sh: I'm back!

Fa: Come on in. I was just dozing off.

Sh: Ah, how do you feel, boy?

So: My headache is gone and I feel lots better. I'm hungry. I'd like some soup. Before this, I felt awful, but I'm even a bit hungry now.

Fa: Fix the boy something, quickly!

Mo: Of course. Some soup. Do you want coffee too?

So: Yes, I'd like both. After I took that medicine, my headache left and I don't have much pain at all any more.

Sh: Good! All you needed was that medicine to set you up!

So: You're right. There's no telling you how happy I'm going to be when I can be back on my feet.

Sh: Don't worry about anything now. I'm going to do my best to make those bad spirits happy that are tormenting you. This is the same thing that always happens when an unclean person walks on the *páramo*. It just makes the *duendes* furious.

So: I believe you. We really behaved disgracefully!

Sh: Don't let it upset you now. You'll get better when I finish my cure.

So: I feel better about everything now. I was worried there for a while that I wasn't going to last much longer.

Sh: I'm sure you were worried. But you're out of danger now. Lie back and rest.

So: I will.

Sh: I'm beat. I'm going home to bed.

So: Fine. I'll eat what they give me and sleep if I can. I do feel much better.

The shaman goes outside and returns to the boy after a few minutes...

Sh: My sensations tell me that you're going to live. You've had all the proper ceremonies done for you, so don't worry about anything.

So: Thank you so much! Now I can relax.

Sh: Goodbye.

Fa: Goodbye. I'll send word tomorrow with someone to let you know how things are going. Or maybe you want to drop by yourself.

Sh: Maybe I'll stop over, since I live so close.

So: I'll keep on eating whatever they offer me. I feel like eating again.

Sh: I don't think you'll have any more problems. The bad spirit has gone to the left. Everything is moving to the right. All my sensations tell me that everything is going toward the right. This is clear indication that your body has accepted the cure.

So: I'm so happy. I can't tell you how much I appreciate what you've done.

Sh: That's all right. See you tomorrow. Goodbye.

Fa: Goodbye. We'll let you know how everything goes.

Sh: Fine. Have a good night.

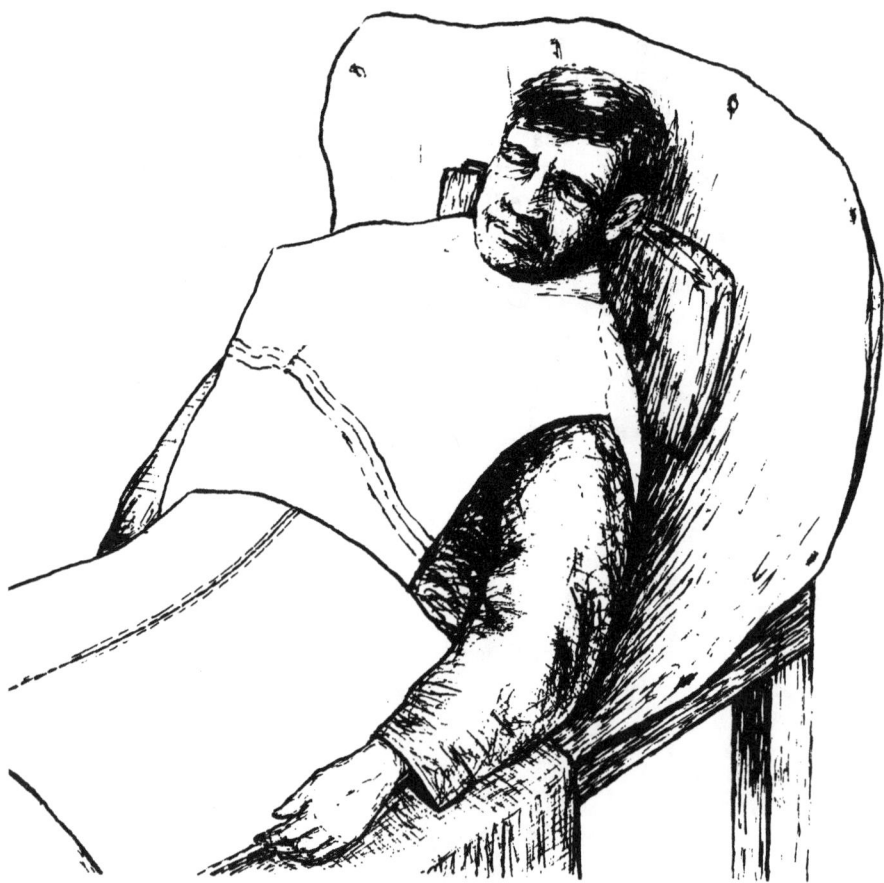

DEATH

Among the Guambianos, death is a major family tragedy. Relatives, neighbors and friends accompany a sick person through his last hours to the point of death, and then on through the night after death occurs. These same people may still be involved for as long as a month after death, in burial and cleansing ceremonies. The ceremonies performed by the church include mass, cemetery burial and prayers in the chapel. Tribal ceremonies come later and involve the removal of deceased's spirit from his house, cleansing of the house and family from contamination, purification and various rituals performed by a shaman.

The family is usually made aware of impending death by the diviner who is called in to cure the patient. If they question the qualifications of that diviner, they will consult others, taking great pains to do everything they can to cure the patient and thus acquit themselves of any responsibility for the death. But if the shamans convince them of unavoidable death, they will stop buying medicines, since it is then obvious that the patient 'doesn't care to live'.

When death does occur, the family immediately purchases a coffin and western clothes for burial. They believe that the sooner they are rid of the deceased's Guambiano clothes, the easier it will be to send his spirit from the house. Some also believe that western clothes will not burn in hell.

The day a person dies, a bier is carried from the chapel in the Guambiano cemetery to the house. Someone from the family is also sent off to Silvia to inform the priest and purchase food for the wake. The deceased is dressed in western clothes, put in the coffin, and laid for viewing in the main room of the house. A small altar is constructed at the head of the coffin to place food, drink, pictures or momentos around the coffin. Family and neighbors arrive to help prepare food, an activity that is now forbidden to the members of the household. The visitors bring gifts of food, firewood, or small amounts of money. Most women help in the kitchen while men accompany the body. The god-children buy large candles to place around the bier where prayer specialists chant at intervals throughout the wake.

The next morning, a mass is held in Silvia or Las Delicias, the Catholic mission station. Then a group led by the dead man's family proceeds to the cemetery. Funerals for the more affluent include prayers by the priest and music played by a hired band from Silvia. Small funerals may consist of around 30 people, while larger ones may be attended by hundreds.

The deceased is placed in a cement vault above ground, called a *bobeda*. Women weep together while the body is cemented into the vault, and then cigarettes and rum are distributed to the guests. Many of the men will get quite drunk, and straggle home as they are able. A period of mourning follows during which the members of deceased's household are prohibited from carrying out routine daily activity.

There is much attention to detail and great financial stress involved in the proper performance of this part of the funeral. But the real focus of Guambiano concern after a death is the deceased's spirit and its effect on the living. Purification ceremonies follow the mourning period of about nine days, when the shaman is called in to send the deceased's spirit from his house. Elaborate ceremonies are performed after the family has searched every corner of the house to remove all of deceased's possessions. Every possible precaution must be taken to rid the house of every trace of the deceased so that his spirit will flee to the 'place of the dead', where it can no longer molest the living.

THE DRAMA OF DEATH

Characters:

Father	*Fa*	Sons	*So*
Mother	*Mo*	Daughters	*Da*
Shaman	*Sh*	Relatives	*Rel*[1] [2] [3] [4]
Grandfather	*Gf*		

SCENE I

In a typical Guambiano home, the old grandfather has taken seriously ill. The family fears his death may be imminent and discusses what should be done...

Fa: It's very possible that our sick father isn't going to recover. What do you think we should do?

Mo: Oh, what will ever become of us if he dies?

Fa: Whatever happens, we'd better get in touch with a diviner.

Mo: Yes, we'd better look for somebody. It's the only thing to do at at time like this. My goodness! Who in the world should we contact? Do you think Joaquin is qualified? We should ask him to see if he would work for us.

Fa: You're right. Why don't you go ask him right away if he'll do this job for us, and take a measure of herbs with you to give him.

Mo: I'll go right now.

Fa: Be sure you tell him we want him to divine very clearly.

Mo: All right.

Fa: Tell him you need to know for certain whether this is a life or death situation.

Mo: All right, I'll ask him. See you later.

Fa: Don't be gone too long. Come right back with word so we'll know which medicine he wants us to get if there's hope for recovery.

Mo: Fine. You wait here.

Fa: Of course. I'll take care of the patient. See you later.

Mother leaves the house. Father walks over to the sick man lying at one end of the room...

> **Fa:** How do you feel?
>
> **Gf:** I can't move a muscle. I feel like my whole body is on fire. It's possible that I just won't make it this time.
>
> **Fa:** Oh, I don't like to hear you talk like that. I've just sent my wife to Joaquin's house to see if he'll divine for us so we'll know how things are going to work out.
>
> **Gf:** Oh, then we'll wait and see what he has to say.
>
> **Fa:** Yes, all we can do is wait.
>
> **Gf:** Who knows if I'll get better or not.
>
> **Fa:** I'm a bit worried myself. Really, the situation wouldn't be so serious if we could find some medicine that would work for you.
>
> **Gf:** I know.
>
> **Fa:** We'll just wait and see what news the wife brings. Would you like to lie down?
>
> **Gf:** Yes, please help me to bed.
>
> **Fa:** Bring your pillow so you'll have two under your head.
>
> **Gf:** Help me lie down so I can rest a while.
>
> **Fa:** We'll just wait until she comes back with instructions, so we'll know what to do for you.
>
> **Gf:** Yes. I'm awfully thirsty.

Father calls to one of his girls...

> **Fa:** Bring some water. Bring boiled brown sugar water.
>
> **Da:** I'll see if there's any made.
>
> **Fa:** Just do what I said!

The girl enters with a bowl of hot sugar water...

> **Fa:** Are you still thirsty, father?
>
> **Gf:** Give me just a sip.
>
> **Fa:** Here, drink all you can.
>
> **Gf:** Thank you.
>
> **Fa:** You should drink more if you can.
>
> **Gf:** Yes, I'll have a little more.

Fa: Have you had enough?

Gf: Save the rest for later.

Fa: Fine.

Gf: Set it down right beside me for later on.

Fa: Let's wait now for the news. Depending on what the diviner says, we should get a *jigra* (ritual bag) ready in case he finds some way to cure this illness.

Gf: Yes, why don't you go ahead and get one ready. Just in case there's hope for my recovery. Let's wait and see what the woman says.

Fa: All right. You stay here and rest. Call me if you want to get up.

Gf: Yes, I'll call if I need anything.

Father moves back to the main part of the house just as his wife returns...

Fa: You're back already!

Mo: Yes.

Fa: Well, what did the diviner have to say?

Mo: I'll tell you word for word what he said: "The patient is either going to live or die. Right now my senses tell me he has a 50-50 chance. There are no sensations on my right. I feel everything on my lower left. It's very possible that the sick man will not recover."

Fa: Oh, what should we do now? Oh, no! I guess the most urgent thing is to get a *jigra* ready to give him when he comes. That's one reason why I was hoping he would come himself. So we'd know for sure what to do.

Mo: Oh, I already told him to come right away. He'll be here any minute.

Fa: I sure hope you got the message straight. The old man is sure to be listening for you and he'll want to know what the diviner said.

Grandfather calls from the other end of the house, and the couple go to his side...

Gf: What did the diviner say? What's the word?

Mo: He said he'd be right over himself.

83

Gf: Oh, that's good. Do you think he'll get here soon?

Mo: I asked him to come just as soon as he could.

Gf: Oh, that's good. In the meantime, I'd like to get up.

Fa: Shall I help you?

Gf: Yes, please.

Mo: Would you like something to drink?

Gf: Yes, a little something would taste good.

Mo: Only God knows if there's any hope for your recovery. In any case, we'll get a *jigra* ready to give Joaquin when he comes.

Gf: You two decide and do what you think best. I'll leave everything up to you.

Fa: We want to do everything in our power to help you get through this illness. We won't overlook anything that might help.

Gf: Oh, me. I feel so depressed about it all.

Fa: Of course you do. But there's nothing we can do for you at this point. We'll just have to wait until Joaquin gets here.

Gf: I know, you're right.

Fa: Let's wait.

A while later, the shaman arrives at the door...

Sh: Anyone home?

Fa: Come right on in.

Sh: You sent for me? I'll be happy to help you in any way I can.

Fa: I can't tell you how much we appreciate your coming. We have a very sick old man here who asked us to send for you.

Sh: I hate to be the one to break this news to you, but I feel that the patient is going to go from bad to worse. This is just between you and me. We mustn't let the old man know he's hanging between life and death.

Fa: Oh, it would be terrible if he didn't recover.

Sh: I understand how you feel. But if it does happen, it's not going to be because you and I didn't do everything in our power to prevent it. So if you folks give your consent, I'd like to act in accordance with what my sensations tell me and my authority as your shaman and try out some of my medicine on him.

Fa: Yes, we should at least try medicine. It's the only thing to do. Also, the old man really wants to know if you think he'll recover, and the medicine might encourage him that you do.

Sh: I'm not offering any false hopes by doing this! Please don't misunderstand. You get a little *jigra* ready. Not any more than what I'll need for one small experiment. Then I'll spend the night in meditation to try to discover what my sensations are telling me. I ask your assistance in this, please. If the time has come for him to die, nothing is going to save him.

Fa: That's right. If it's his time to die, there's not a thing either of us can do, no matter how much we'd like to save him.

Sh: I agree. Now please get the *jigra* ready while I run home for the medicine I need. You all wait here. I'll be right back.

Fa: Fine, but please don't be gone long.

Sh: No, I'll be right back. You all wait for me.

About an hour passes. The shaman goes to his house for medicinal herbs and returns to begin work...

Sh: All right. I'm back and ready to work.

Fa: Good. I'm glad you could get right back.

Sh: Now then, do you have the *jigra* ready?

Fa: Yes, everything is all set.

Sh: Fill it with these things: five dollars, a bottle of rum, three measures of herbs and four packs of cigarettes.

Fa: All right.

Sh: Please give me a pinch of herbs. I'm going to divine first of all.

Fa: Do you have something to put it in? Here, I'll put it right in your hand.

Sh: Just a little pinch. Now wait a second. The first thing I want to do is take these herbs and divine whether the old man will live or die.

85

Fa: Yes, please do that first thing.

Sh: Now give me the *jigra*.

Mo: I have it right here. We've got to use every means possible to save his life. But if it's his time to die, there's not a thing any of us can do about it.

Sh: Obviously. I'm only giving medicine as an experiment. I feel very definitely in my senses that nothing is going to work. If my sensations won't move from my left side to my right and things look absolutely irreversible, I'm only going to work until nine or ten o'clock. If all indications point to an unfavorable outcome, I'll let you know. But don't say anything about any of this to the old man.

Fa: Of course not.

Sh: Now I'm going to sit down outside and get to work.

Fa: Yes, go right ahead.

A few minutes later, the shaman rushes into the house as he hears a commotion...

Mo: Oh dear. What a terrible, terrible shame. What a tragedy!

Fa: Is he dead?

Mo: Yes, he's dead!

Sh: I knew this would happen. I predicted that he was a hopeless case.

Fa: You were right. What should we do? We need to take things calmly. He's dead. We'll need to get together to make plans for the burial.

So: I'll go call everyone that isn't here already to come right over.

Fa: Well, do it quickly. Tell the whole family and all the relatives that the old man is dead. We have to make plans to go to Silvia. Oh, this is terrible! I just knew it would happen. What a tragedy! But we must bear up. It's all over now. He's dead.

Mo: I just had a feeling this tragedy would fall on us.

Fa: We'll get the family together to plan for the burial and other necessities like his suit, the casket... We want to have everything ready. Son, go quickly.

So: All right, father.

The boy leaves to spread word of the old man's death. Some time passes, and the family and relatives begin to arrive one by one...

Fa: He's dead.

Rel: You can't mean it. He's really dead?

Fa: Yes. What shall we do? We did everything we could to save his life, but it was all in vain. What are we going to do? We need to get the family together and decide what we should do first. We need food and so many others things for the funeral.

Rel: I know!

Rel[1]: He's really dead, then? I'm so sorry.

Rel[2]: What's happened here?

Rel[3]: Oh, what shall we do? He's dead!

Rel[4]: I was afraid this would happen any day now.

Fa: There's nothing more we can do for him. We tried hard to save him, but our efforts were futile. Ah, my, it's all over!

So: Somebody should get going down to Silvia. How many of us do you think should go?

Fa: I think four of you would be enough. Buy burial clothes, and be sure you get the right size. Get shoes, a shirt, tie, and anything else you think of that we'll need.

So: Fine.

Fa: While you're there, get the groceries we need for the wake—*panela* (raw sugar), rice and coffee.

So: All right.

Fa: We'll bury him tomorrow.

So: Yes.

Fa: Now that his days on earth have ended, there's nothing else we can do for him. We'll bury him tomorrow.

Rel: It all seems unreal. But we'll do what we have to. We'll come back a little later.

Fa: Yes, you do that. Each one of you keep in mind everything we need. You boys don't go and forget something important.

So: Don't worry about us.

> *Fa:* O.K. See you later. Get back here as soon as you can.

The sons leave for Silvia. Relatives return home to get items the family will need for the wake. They all return to the house later that night...

> *Mo:* Oh, you're back.
> *So:* Yes. Is Dad here?
> *Fa:* I'm right here.
> *So:* Come here a minute. You know what? We forgot candles!
> *Fa:* Well, you'll just have to go right back and get them. And the rest of you need to go bring the *camagracia* (bier).
> *Rel:* All right. Let's go.
> *Fa:* Does everyone understand what needs to be done?
> *So:* Yes. Everyone has agreed to help out and do what needs to be done.
> *Fa:* Good. Let's all work together.

The family and relatives scatter again to see to the many details of the wake and burial. Several more hours pass...

> *So:* It looks like everyone is back. We've got to dress the old man. Dad, come here! Who's going to dress the old man in his burial suit?
> *Mo:* The man's sons should do it. Samuel, you come put the suit on your father. Bring Manuel to help you. We want him all ready before people start coming.
> *Fa:* All right. There. He's ready now. Where's the casket?
> *So:* The boys should be here with it any minute.
> *Fa:* I sure hope they hurry.
> *Rel[1]:* Have they finished dressing the old man?
> *Rel[2]:* Yes. He's all ready.
> *Fa:* Do you see anyone coming with the casket?
> *So:* Here they are with it now.
> *Fa:* Then let's get the body in the casket so everything is ready when people start arriving.
> *Rel[1]:* Good. Here's the casket.
> *Fa:* Carry it over here. Some of you others come help

us lift the body into the casket. Come right over here. Please help me lift him into the casket. Thanks. Put pillows around him. Is everything in place?

So: Yes, he looks just right, perfect. Shall we put his ponchos around him?

Fa: If they're new ones. Let's put them behind his head, then the pillows on top of the ponchos. Bring them here. Now, wife, daughters, gather around me.

The mother and her daughters weep together at the casket...

Mo and Da: Oh, Father! Oh, grandfather!

Fa: I guess that's everything. We can put the lid on tomorrow.

So: Yes, we can nail it shut first thing in the morning.

Fa: We'll carry him into the main room now. Bring the *camagracia*.

So: It's all ready, right here.

Fa: Then four of you please carry the casket into the living room.

*Four of the relatives carry the casket on the **camagracia** into the main room of the house where it is placed for viewing the body...*

So: That looks good, right there.

Fa: Does the casket fit? You're sure it's not too big for the *camagracia*?

So: It's perfect. It's just the right size.

Fa: Then please put the *camagracia* down right over here.

So: All right. It looks fine right there.

The men continue to fuss over the casket, setting it at just the right angle...

Fa: Now all of you who have already done so much, please stay and help out in any way you can.

Rel: Don't worry about anything. We're all anxious to do all we can to help you.

Fa: I invite you all to accompany us for the rest of the night. Tomorrow is the funeral.

Rel: We'll all go home and get something to help out with the wake.

> *Fa:* I beg all of you to stay with us tonight. I really
> appreciate having you here.
>
> *Rel:* Don't worry about anything. We'll be back later.

*Those who haven't already brought something to the house leave to
secure gifts of potatoes, coffee, rice, **panela** (raw sugar), and
firewood to help in feeding those who gather for the night-long
wake. They will slip small gifts of money into a bag the man of
the house wears on his shoulder for the occasion...*

> *Fa:* Now then, tomorrow we'll carry the casket down the
> mountain for the funeral. We'll leave here with the
> body around eight o'clock.
>
> *So:* Since this separation will last forever, we should do
> the very best we can for the old man. We should
> invite the band to play for the funeral.
>
> *Fa:* Good idea!
>
> *So:* There's no reason why we shouldn't. Grandpa has
> everything provided for, so we could afford the band.
> He left cows, horses, land, even a little money.
> There's plenty to hire the band.
>
> *Fa:* Then we'll hire the band! Now, tomorrow at eight
> o'clock, we need to be in Silvia for the mass.
>
> *So:* We'll work out details with the priest and musicians;
> we'll have everything ready when you get there.

*After watching through the night with the body, the family and
guests leave at daybreak for Silvia. The sound of a funeral procession moving down the mountain may be felt before it is heard. The
ground vibrates as any number from 50 to 100 people run down
the steep trail with the casket. The group is led by deceased's
family to the church in Silvia.*

SCENE II

*Outside the Catholic church on the plaza in Silvia, the family and guests gather
to await the funeral mass...*

> *Fa:* All right now, the priest told me he'd say mass at
> ten o'clock.
>
> *So:* Good. We'll be ready. Let's carry the body into the
> church. Please ask someone to help carry the casket.

Rel: We'll do whatever you tell us.

The family enters the church carrying the casket...

So: It looks like everyone is here.
Fa: The priest has just arrived. He's beginning the mass. See that everyone comes inside to hear mass.

SCENE III

On the street from the church to the cemetery...

Fa: Are you sure you told the band what time to come?
So: Yes, they promised to be here. There are twelve of them coming to play.
Fa: What did they ask?
So: Three hundred fifty. We settled on that if they'd play from the church to the cemetery.
Fa: It looks like we're ready. The band is arriving. Let's go. Let's begin the prayers. There are five stops for prayer between here and the bridge.
So: All of you in the band, please join the procession to the cemetery. We've agreed on your fee, so please play for the procession.
Band: Fine. Don't worry about anything.

The band plays...

Fa: Please help carry the casket, everyone. Don't just let the willing ones do all the work.

More music plays. The procession begins to move...

Fa: I invite you all to accompany us. Everyone please take a turn carrying the body.

The band plays, someone sings...

See how the family mourns the loss of their father.
Poor people! They've been left all alone.
The old man has bid farewell to his sons.
We're marching to the cemetery.
We're marching to the cemetery.

Fa: Please, everyone, cooperate and help carry the body. This is the last time I'll need to ask you this favor. Everyone please help! We're almost there!

So much grief, this separation from our father.
Just this one day, please, everyone, stay with me.
I'm grief-stricken over my father's death
I never thought it would really happen
Nobody thought Father would ever die.

Fa: Please help carry the casket! We're about to enter the cemetery. Musicians, one last number, please!

So much grief over your father.
Here we are in the place of the dead
Now that you are to take his place
Follow in your good father's footsteps.

So it's farewell, farewell, farewell, farewell, farewell my sons;
Farewell, farewell all you people. Farewell, farewell, world.
Farewell, farewell, farewell friends, farewell.

DISMISSING DECEASED'S SPIRIT

Following the death and burial of a Guambiano, ceremonies continue in the home of the deceased to get his spirit to leave the world of the living. These spirits are feared to have dangerous powers which cause sickness or death by attracting away the souls of the living. A shaman is called in to cleanse the house, family and possessions, and to dismiss the dangerous spirit from its former home.

Usually, the family first contacts a diviner in the neighborhood who will then recommend a specialist powerful enough to send away spirits of the dead. One of the men of the house will visit the local shaman, taking a gift of money, herbs, rum and tobacco. During the negotiations, the family will need to obligate the shaman to the point where he feels that his reputation will not be damaged in the event he fails to get rid of the spirit. The family will settle with the shaman on what items he will need to do his work, in accordance with the influence the deceased had in the community and the power of his lingering spirit.

The family then gathers all the old clothing, bench, bed, and other personal possessions of deceased and places them in a pile outside the house when the shaman arrives. He and his assistant then each receive a *jigra*, or woven carrying-bag, containing the items they agreed on to perform the ceremony. They drink rum, chew herbs, and begin the long process of cleansing the house of signs of the spirit's presence. The chief shaman carries a black bamboo staff which is his sign of authority over the spirit world.

The ritual may go on for hours while the specialists drink, chew and consult about their sensations. The principle shaman is responsible for dismissing the spirit, purifying the house and family. His assistant is concerned mainly with his sensations. He must be consulted throughout the entire ceremony regarding his sensations before the chief shaman is satisfied that the course of events is moving smoothly. Feelings on the left indicate that evil influence is still overpowering the issue, while feelings on the right indicate that the ritual is having the desired effect.

Both the shaman and his assistant blow a mixture of rum and herbs over the house, inside and out, as they brush the floor with stinging nettles inside and all around the house. The remaining rooms are also cleansed of traces of the spirit. If wailing or squeaking noises are heard, or something else interferes with the shaman's sensations, a search is made for items belonging to the deceased that may have been overlooked when his things were cleaned out. When the shaman is finally satisfied that the spirit has left the house, he then cleanses the family members who have been ritually contaminated up to this point. The pile of deceased's belongings is then burned or thrown off a high cliff into the river to discourage the spirit from returning.

The family and relatives celebrate after the ceremonies are completed until dawn, drinking with the shaman to a job well done and signalling to the community the closing of their negotiations with him in the purification of their dwelling. The family, also free from contamination, prepare a meal for everyone.

A second cleansing may take place several weeks after the first one. This may be done as a precaution against the spirit's returning, or it may be because strange noises indicate that the spirit never left. The same procedures are then repeated and the family again returns to a normal round of activities, which may the include working the deceased's fields and using some of his possessions that were too valuable to destroy.

THE DRAMA OF DISMISSING DECEASED'S SPIRIT

Characters:

Father	*Fa*	Sons	*So*¹ ² ³
Mother	*Mo*	Shaman	*Sh*
Household	*Ho*	Shaman's Wife	*SW*
Uncles	*Un*	Shaman's Assistant	*SA*
Daughters	*Da*		

SCENE I

At the house of the deceased grandfather and his family, the funeral is over. Now the cleansing ceremonies must be taken care of to dismiss his lingering spirit from the family dwelling. They must contact a shaman and negotiate with him to perform this function for them...

Fa: We need to make some plans. Who do you think we should get in touch with about capturing Grandfather's spirit?

Mo: I just don't know who would be best. I've known too many people who spend all their money on cleansing ceremonies only to find out that the spirit is still there. Who knows who you can count on these days to do a good job.

Fa: I know what you mean. Let's check with Trino first. He appeals to me as an expert on these matters. But let's check out his qualifications with someone who knows him better, first. Why don't you go over to Manuel's and ask him to divine whether or not Trino is powerful enough to dismiss spirits.

So¹: I'll go. How much money and herbs do you think the advice is worth?

Fa: For this, I don't think you should have to pay more than one measure of herbs and a dollar.

So¹: Well, give me whatever you think he'll ask and I'll go see what he has to say.

Mo: Just a minute. I'll get things ready for you.

So¹: I'm leaving now to see what Manuel has to say.

Fa: Well, be sure you tell him we want a good job done on the divinations. We want someone who's qualified.

So¹: Naturally. Do you have the *jigra* ready, Mother?

Mo: One dollar, 2 cigarettes, one measure of herbs and a small bottle of rum. I guess that should be plenty of everything.

So¹: Good. I'll be back later.

Fa: Now be sure you tell him we want a good job on the divinations. We need to know what to do.

So¹: Right. I'll be back later.

Fa: All right. There he goes. Let's wait and see what advice he brings back. If he comes back with word that Manuel thinks he's qualified himself to catch the spirit, then we can go ahead and hire him. I don't know how much rum, herbs and other things we have on hand. We might even have to get our hands on some cash. It all depends on what he finds out. Look, there are four of us sons of the old man here. We should work this out together. One of us can buy the herbs, another the rum, and the others chip in with money.

Un: We'll do our part.

Fa: Let's wait and see what the boy has to say.

So²: I think I'll run over to Manuel's too and find out what's going on.

Fa: Well, don't be gone long.

So²: All right.

About an hour passes...

Fa: That looks like the boys coming back now. Yes, here they come. Let's see what they have to say. Depending on their message, we could still contact Trino and send him a *jigra* of medicine to appease the spirit yet tonight. Did everything go all right, son?

So¹: Yes. He said that if we thought we could pay Trino a big enough fee to make it worth his while, he would be the best qualified to do the job.

Fa: Of course, I knew all the time that Trino's qualifications were good. So, now, go over to Trino's and tell him I would like to see him. Don't tell him anything more. Just that I want to see him.

So¹: He's probably not even home this time of day.

Fa: He might be there. Now get going and don't waste any more time.

So¹: Oh, all right!

The son leaves the house to contact the principle shaman, Trino...

Fa: Let's wait and see what happens. Now that we know Trino is powerful enough to çatch dead spirits, we must insist that he do the job for us, no matter how many excuses he might give us for not wanting to.

The son returns a while later...

Fa: What did he say? Was he home or not?

So¹: Yes, he was home.

Fa: Is he coming over?

So¹: He said he was busy now, but he might drop by later.

Fa: What in the world has he got to do that's so important? I've got to know right now if he can be hired. Go back over there and tell him we have to see him right away.

So¹: Oh, all right!

Fa: If you can, bring him back with you. Plead with him!

So¹: Whatever you say.

The son leaves the house again and his father paces at the door...

So²: That looks like him coming back now!

Fa: Look out and see if Trino's with him.

So²: Yes, he's right behind him.

Fa: Great!

The elder son enters the house with the shaman at his heels...

Sh: Good afternoon.

Fa: Come right in!

Sh: Your son tells me you want to see me. So I'm here. I came to see how I could be of service to you.

Fa: That was very nice of you. I sent my son to call

you because we have a case we'd like for you to handle for us.

Sh: Oh?

Fa: First, though, come on inside and sit in the kitchen with us.

Sh: Thank you.

Fa: Wait just a minute and my wife will bring you some supper.

Sh: I appreciate it.

Fa: We've heard that you're an expert at dismissing spirits from homes of the dead. We sent for you with the intention of asking you to catch the spirit in this house. We had another specialist in mind, but decided that we'd prefer to have you purify our house. I'm thinking about having you come appease the spirit tonight, if you could.

Sh: You'll have to excuse me. I do have other things to do. I'm not at all sure I'm the man you want for this job.

Fa: I beg you to listen to me. There really isn't anyone else we know to ask. I'll admit I asked another specialist for his opinion about you and he sent word back with my sons that you were the best qualified to work for us. You do it for everyone else!

Sh: I don't know what to say. I'm afraid I just don't have the time right now.

Fa: Please help me. To be perfectly frank with you, I don't know what else to do. There isn't anyone else to ask.

Sh: Who would you get to assist me?

Fa: We were thinking of hiring Manuel.

Sh: Oh, him! I suppose he's fairly well-qualified. But I have a feeling this spirit is very powerful. The dead man was very influential in this community. Removing his spirit from this house would be a formidable job for anyone to tackle.

Fa: But you have such a reputation for handling these spirits, and I beg you to help me. Isn't there any possibility at all that you could do this purification for us?

Sh: All right, I'll do it. But only because you're on the spot and can't get anyone else.

Fa: Good! Now that you've agreed, what's your fee? How much money, herbs and rum do you want in your *jigra*?

Sh: Hold on a minute there! The first thing I have to do is check out my sensations. Good grief! This really is a strong spirit. If we only use small quantities of medicine, this one is going to get away from us. I just don't know. I have a feeling this spirit could be bigger that I am. It almost overpowers my sensations. I'm not at all sure I can handle it.

Fa: Shall we round up more herbs and rum?

Sh: If what you have on hand isn't enough, it's just possible that this spirit will completely overpower me!

Fa: Don't worry about that. We'll provide whatever you ask for.

Sh: I should hope so! All right. Tonight I'll need a half pound of herbs, a half litre of rum and five dollars. I have other medicines at home. I'd better get to work. Wait for me while I go home for what I need.

Fa: We'll wait. Should we be getting the *jigra* ready with the items you mentioned?

Sh: Yes. Be sure my *jigra* contains rum, herbs, and five dollars. You'll need another one for my assistant with three measures of herbs, half a litre of rum and three dollars.

Fa: All right.

The shaman leaves for home to gather up the tools of his profession...

SCENE II

In the shaman's house, he informs his wife that he has contracted to do a job. He hurries out to look for herbs...

Sh: Well, my good wife. That family I just went to see begged me to work for them. I had to give in.

There's no one else to take care of them.

SW: I know how it is. You really have no other choice,
do you?

Sh: I'm going to have to make a quick trip up the
mountain to hunt for the three herbs I'll need. I don't
have anything on hand because I wasn't expecting a
job like this. But there isn't any big problem. I
should be able to find the herbs growing fairly close
by.

SW: Well, don't be gone too long or it will be very late
before you get back to their house.

SCENE III

*Back at the house of the deceased grandfather, the shaman returns with his
herbs ready to begin work. It is cold and dark outside. Night shadows cast by the
mountains make a fitting backdrop for this scene...*

Sh: Here I am again. Do you have the *jigras* ready?

Fa: Come right in. We've got everything ready.

Sh: Has someone contacted Manuel?

Fa: Yes. He sent word that he'd be over to assist you.

Sh: In the meantime, I'm going to start work. Someone
go tell Manuel to get here as soon as he can. The
bad spirit seems to be arriving.

Fa: (To one of his sons...) Hurry up and tell him to get
right over here.

*The son leaves and brings Manuel to the house a few minutes
later...*

Sh: (To Manuel) It looks like we've got our work cut
out for us. I'm glad you're here to assist me.

SA: Yes. They begged me to come over and help you. I
couldn't get out of it. I finally had to accept.

Sh: I know how it goes. I appreciate your coming.
Here's the *jigra* they fixed for you.

SA: Oh, good.

Sh: I have a sensation on my right that tells me this is a
very brave spirit.

SA: Oh, brother!

Sh: The dead man was very courageous. It looks like he and his spirit were two of a kind. Let's chew the herbs and blow them around with a little rum.

SA: Right. If we aren't careful to do everything correctly, this one might get away from us.

Sh: We're going to have to have a lot more than they've given us to work tonight. For you, half a pound of herbs and half a litre of rum. For me, three quarters of a litre of rum and three quarters of a pound of herbs. If we use all this, my sensations tell me the spirit will flee away. I feel this issue on my right and not on the left. They've got to go through the house soon and collect all the dead man's possessions—hoes, machetes, money, everything—and put it all in one pile.

SA: Right.

Sh: Let's get to work. I want all of you in this family to stay right here in the house and nobody step out that door. The spirits of the living interfere with our work.

Fa: All right. Go ahead and work. Don't worry about us.

The shaman and his assistant go outside the house for the first hour or so of the ceremony. It gets late...

Sh: It must be around ten o'clock.

SA: Yes, that would be my guess, too.

Sh: Let's call the man of the house. We're missing something. They might be asleep in there. Go see if you can wake up anyone.

Manuel calls at the door. One of the daughters steps out to see what they need...

Sh: Are you sure you got absolutely everything out of the house that belonged to the old man? Something is interfering with my work. The only thing I can figure is that something of the old man's must still be in the house.

Da: We've cleaned out absolutely everything.

Sh: There's something right in the middle of the house that is jamming my sensations and attracting the spirit back inside. The spirit just reaches the point of leaving, then goes back in there, walks around the four corners of the house and settles down in the middle of the room. He gets away from me every time. You must search again very carefully.

The mother overhears the shaman and comes to the door...

Mo: My word, whatever could be in that room?

Sh: Well, it's something that's really jamming my vibrations. Light a couple of candles and check up in the rafters. Are you sure there isn't an old carrying bag of grandfather's hanging around somewhere in that room?

Da: You're right! I did see a bag hanging in there!

Mo: You climb up and look around in the rafters to see what you can find. I'll look in all the bags down here. You look as hard as you can for anything that might have been your grandfather's up there.

Da: There's nothing in the rafters.

Mo: It looks like a handkerchief, or something in this bag! Look! A handkerchief! It's the old man's life savings! Go tell Trino we found the old man's money in the bottom of his old carrying-bag.

The daughter runs outside to inform the shaman. He enters the house to have a look for himself...

Sh: See there now! Every time the spirit came around, he moved right to that spot. This was getting in our way every time. Now, put all the money and clothes, or anything else you find of the old man's in that pile over there on the left.

Da: I will.

The shaman exits and resumes his work with Manuel...

Sh: Now my sensations are coming on the right. Watch it now! I don't want the spirit to get away to the left. Everything is vibrating on my right. There's no feeling at all on the left. It was that money that was fouling things up for us. If we hadn't discovered it, we might have worked our heads off for three nights all for nothing. This always happens when they leave something lying around belonging to the dead person. The spirit won't leave his belongings. Pay close attention now to your sensations and see if the spirit is taking the right course, or if there's still something interfering. Look, there comes the spirit! Just a minute ago I heard it wailing, looking for someplace to go. It makes me feel just awful, but we have to keep after it. All you people in the house stay right where you are. Get together in one spot. I'm coming in.

Ho: All right!

Sh: Manuel, you stay right where you are and keep tabs on the sensations so nothing goes wrong. I'm going in after the spirit. I'll chase it down and beat it with stinging nettles.

SA: O.K. I'll keep things under control at this end.

Sh: After I circle the room inside four times, I'll come back out to see if the spirit has passed by you on the way out. Keep your eyes open. Everything depends on your sensations at this stage of the game.

SA: All right.

Sh: Here goes!

SA: Do your best!

The shaman enters the house...

Sh: Don't anyone move! I feel terrible about what I have to do. Your grandfather was my friend, but I have to chase his spirit until it leaves. Bring me a bowl of water and set it in the doorway. I'll stand back and see if the spirit comes for a drink.

Mother goes to the kitchen for a bowl of water and returns with it...

Mo: Where do you want it?

Sh: Set it down right there, and then move out of the way quickly. I want everyone to stay over on the left side because I'm going after the spirit. It makes me sad to have to do it. The old man was a relative of mine. But there's nothing I can do about that now. I have to whip the spirit until he moves in the right direction. Watch it! Look out! That's the first time around, and that's the second. I need to chase it from the four corners of the room and whip it with nettles so it won't settle down again somewhere. Now I've finished two rounds. I'm going outside to consult my assistant. Are you out there, Manuel?

The shaman goes outside to talk with Manuel...

SA: I'm over here.
Sh: Oh, very good. I have to make four rounds through the house. I've just done two and need to do two more. Good. I don't think there's going to be any problem. The spirit is moving in the right direction. What a job! You go inside this time and bring me what I need. I want my bottle of rum.
SA: Anything you say.
Sh: Take this bottle of rum and have three shots to fortify yourself. I don't want you getting scared on me.
SA: All right. I'll pour you one, too.
Sh: Yes, I'll have a little. There's not much left in my bottle.

The shaman's assistant enters the house to refill the rum bottles. The shaman and his assistant then drink together...

SA: All right. You're ready now to go back in there and give it all you have. Relax! I don't see any problems. Everything is moving along smoothly.

The shaman re-enters the house...

Sh: I started at the door, went around the four corners of the room and ended up in the middle. Then I went outside, blew medicine all around, swept the ground good with stinging nettles—everything possible to get the spirit to move out. Have any of you heard noises coming from the kitchen or any other rooms?
Ho: No. Nobody has heard a sound.
Sh: Then I'm going through the whole house one more time. Put all the dishes together in one place. I'm going to the kitchen to cleanse the corners of that

room. Gather everything up and then get everyone out of the way so I can do my work.

Fa: Get everything gathered up. Good, he's coming out to the kitchen. Now he's chasing the spirit out of the kitchen.

Sh: Are you sure nobody has heard any noises? When the spirit hides in a corner, it makes squeaking noises. Nothing?

Fa: Nothing. Just a minute ago I saw what I thought was a white dog around the pile of grandfather's stuff. To tell you the truth, I didn't pay much attention to whether it was really a dog or not. I saw it move around the pile, but I thought it was just the neighbor's dog. Do you think it could have been the spirit?

Sh: Of course! It must have been the spirit! I'll take one last look around. Everything looks good. I'm going to whip the spirit one last time. I just hate to treat an old neighbor like this. I didn't want this job in the first place. Your grandfather was my friend. Commanding it away makes me feel like his enemy. But I don't have any choice. You made me do it for you.

Fa: Don't worry. We're only doing what has to be done. It's the way we've always done things. We can't let the old man's spirit stay around. Don't worry about it. You're only doing your job.

Sh: I know you're right, but that doesn't make it any easier on me. I'm all finished inside here now. Two times around the outside of the house to chase the spirit toward his pile of things again. From there I have to be explicit about sending it on the right path to flee into eternity. I'll indicate the direction with my black staff, whip it with stinging nettles and everything else I have to do to get it going. That way, it will flee to its own place because its time has come. Manuel!

SA: You called?

Sh: Yes, you stand right here and watch closely just in case the spirit gets away from me. I'm going to chase it away from his pile of things. I'll do whatever has to be done to dismiss it from this house and send it to its own place. Manuel, are you having any problems? The spirit didn't get away to your left, did it?

SA: No!

Sh: We're on the right track now. There's nothing more I can do. The spirit has left now. I've done everything in the book and instructed it where to go. I blew all the herbs around the house, outside and inside where he kept his things. It's gone! It's gone! I don't feel anything in my senses. Nothing on the right, nothing on the left. It's gone!

Fa: Oh, thank you. We're grateful to you for all you've done.

Sh: What a shame. He's gone. I feel so let down.

Fa: In a case like this, it was the only thing you could do.

Sh: Well, anyway, my job is finished. I'm grateful to all of you for your cooperation. Now I'm going to serve each of you a shot of the rum we had left over. Please bring me a glass.

Fa: (To wife...) Go find a glass. There's one in the kitchen somewhere. Go get it.

Mo: Here!

Sh: Everyone join me for a drink of the rum we have left after the long night's work.

Ho: Thank you.

Sh: First the man of the house. The rest of you will all get a turn.

Fa: Thank you.

Sh: You boys there, come over here. Drink some of what we had left over.

So[1] [2] [3]: Thank you.

Fa: All of my relatives and you specialists, too, please stay and spend the night with us. Don't leave yet.

Sh: All right. I'll share my left-over rum with you, my friends.

Fa: I've got another bottle. It's a gift for you.

experts. Now, everyone pass the bottle around. We'll all be drunk by morning. Some of you might make it home, but the rest can sleep it off here.

Several hours pass. Dawn will break soon. Father is very drunk, but still hosting his housefull of guests...

Fa: I'd like to give you all another drink, but I'm completely out of rum. We've drunk everything I have. We'll get some food ready for everyone. Women, hurry up and fix us all something to eat. I want to share a meal with all our good friends!

SIL International Publications
Additional Releases in the **The International Museum of Cultures Publications in Ethnology Series**

41. **The Norsk Høstfest: A celebration of ethnic food and ethnic identity,** by Paul Thomas Emch, 2011, 121 pp., ISBN 978-1-55671-265-4.

40. **Our company increases apace: History, language, and social identity in early colonial Andover, Massachucetts,** by Elinor Abbot, 2007, 279 pp., ISBN 978-1-55671-169-5.

39. **What place for hunters-gatherers in millenium three?** by Thomas N. Headland and Doris E. Blood, eds. 2002, 130 pp., ISBN 978-1-55671-132-9.

38. **A tale of Pudicho's people,** by Richard Montag. 2002, 181 pp., ISBN 978-1-55671-131-2.

37. **African friends and money matters,** by David E. Maranz, 2001, 237 pp., ISBN 1-55671-117-4.

36. **The value of the person in the Guahibo culture,** by Marcelino Sosa, translated by Walter del Aguila, 1999, 158 pp., ISBN 978-1-55671-085-8.

35. **People of the drum of God—Come!,** by Paul Neeley, 1999, 310 pp., ISBN 978-1-55671-013-1.

34. **Cashibo folklore and culture: Prose, poetry, and historical background,** by Lila Wistrand-Robinson, 1998, 196 pp., ISBN 978-1-55671-048-3.

SIL International Publications
7500 W. Camp Wisdom Road
Dallas, TX 75236-5629

Voice: 972-708-7404
Fax: 972-708-7363
publications_intl@sil.org
www.ethnologue.com/bookstore.asp